S. S. Smith
Res.

J. Morris

J. Fairland

J. Guthile
E. Morris
J. Sennett
J. Wiffley

GREAT NECK

TOWN OF NORTH HEMPSTEAD

Scale 40 Rods to the inch

Store
S. E. Hayden
A. Hiller

J. Studer

B. S. Sh.

SCHOOL N.º 7

C. H. Baxter
H. Allen
J. Brewer
N. Hayden
Store &

J. Bender
Wheelwright Sh.

J. Brewer
Store

J. Brewer

FREE CHURCH

Temperance Hall
G. H. Smith
H. Lahr
E. R. Gillar
J. M. Carpenter
C. Austin

J. Brewer

H. K. Hayden
M. P. Baker

TM DESIGN'S

ULTIMATE BOOK

OF

GREAT NECK

Fabled Tales & Fabulous Images

Page III - Rake Boy ca. 1915 Thomaston, house #114 built by Thomas Shrieve and house # 124 moved from Northern Blvd.
This Page - Tom Thurston's Blacksmith Shop, Middle Neck Road. South of Present Post Office, ca. 1899

TM DESIGN'S

ULTIMATE BOOK
OF

GREAT
NECK

Fabled Tales

&

Fabulous Images

WRITTEN BY

MARCELLE S.
FISCHLER

TM Design's Ultimate Book of Great Neck
Fabled Tales & Fabulous Images

Written By
MARCELLE S. FISCHLER

Publisher / Editor / Digital Art / Photography
GLENN BUCALO

Assistant to Publisher
SALLY BURRIESCI

Digital Art
JOSEPH REICHENBACH

Advertising Sales Consultant
RENEE OWENS

Research Assistant
DANIEL S. FISCHLER

Very Special Thanks:
Anthony N. Carbone - *for introducing the book
concept and having a clear and definite belief in
and appreciation for Target Marketing & Design.*

Elliot S. Rosenblatt - *for his relentless efforts and
dedication to the success of this book.*

Also special thanks to:
Risha Rosner, Leila Mattson, Linda Emanuel,
Regina Gil, David Lurie, Laurie Kutscera, Nick
Kutscera, Bali Singh, Joshua Ruff, Lara
Silberklang, Freda Sussman, Charles Sussman,
Serge Fischler, and all the advertisers whose sup-
port made this book possible.

TM DESIGN
A division of Target Marketing & Design, Inc.
(631) 226-5234
www.tmdesign.net

Cover Photograph - Grace Building and Middle Neck Road,
Station Plaza North

Waiting for the Steamboat, the end Steamboat Road - ca. 1800's

Old Bathing Beach - near Steamboat Landing - now the U.S. Merchant Marine Academy, ca. 1920's

Dear Friends:

   The Great Neck Chamber of Commerce takes great pride in presenting "The Ultimate Book of Great Neck." Never before has such a compilation of words and images of Great Neck been put together in one source! We hope it will be a valuable resource for capturing Great Neck's interesting past along with todays fabulous restaurants, unique stores and boutiques, and invigorating and relaxing salons and spas. Great Neck is also known for the variety and quality of its professionals. In Great Neck, personal care, attention and service are at an unsurpassed level. Spend some time in Great Neck where you can partake of culinary delights, be pampered and enjoy a unique shopping experience on Long Island.

   Our thanks to Target Marketing & Design, Inc., and especially to Glenn Bucalo for his creativity, vision, enthusiasm and phenomenal attention to detail, and to Renee Owens for her energy and perseverance in presenting the concept of the book to the Great Neck business community and to Marcelle S. Fischler for writing the book.

   We encourage you to utilize the advertisers and retain the book for its wonderful photos and history of Great Neck. We thank the businesses whose support has made this book possible. They have shown their commitment to our community by promoting a strong and vibrant economic environment.

   This book brings to life the history, memories and contemporary expressions of Great Neck. I am confident you will agree that this book epitomizes what we already know: Great Neck is a wonderful place to live, work and shop!

Sincerely,

Elliot S. Rosenblatt

Elliot S. Rosenblatt
President
Great Neck Chamber of Commerce

CONTENTS

28

49

118

Frank Lloyd Wright H

74

113

48

42

109

44

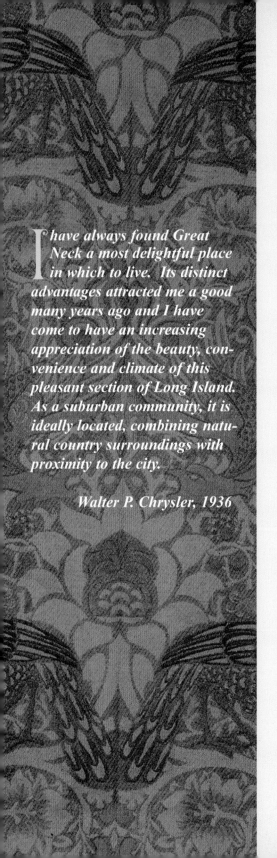

I have always found Great Neck a most delightful place in which to live. Its distinct advantages attracted me a good many years ago and I have come to have an increasing appreciation of the beauty, convenience and climate of this pleasant section of Long Island. As a suburban community, it is ideally located, combining natural country surroundings with proximity to the city.

Walter P. Chrysler, 1936

INTRODUCTION:
A PLACE TO CALL HOME

Great Neck has always been the kind of the place where people wanted to live. With top-ranked schools, expansive parks, well-stocked libraries, beautiful homes, lush properties and an easy commute to Manhattan, the fabled peninsula has a small town feel yet exudes a sophistication and a vitality of life unique on Long Island and in suburban America. It is one of the most remarkable residential communities in the world.

Divided into nine villages and some unincorporated areas in the town of North Hempstead in Nassau County, Great Neck is anything but another cookie cutter bedroom colony. Its population is affluent; its aura exudes success. Every street is prime, many lined with towering 100-year-old trees.

The heart of Long Island's Gold Coast, Great Neck's history is rich with star-spangled tales of success. It was in Great Neck, of course, that F. Scott Fitzgerald found the inspiration to write the American classic, *The Great Gatsby*. It was in Great Neck that the famed *Yankee Doodle Dandy* composer George M. Cohan also wrote *45 Minutes from Broadway*, that Oscar Hammerstein II created some of his greatest music and business magnates like Walter Percy Chrysler, William K. Vanderbilt Jr. and builder Alfred Levitt chose to live.

From Lake Success to the south to Kings Point at the northernmost tip, Great Neck is a vibrant and bustling community, teeming with cultural, civic and religious organizations and activities. Its population is diverse: Mostly white and heavily Jewish, Great Neck has a unique blend of Persian, Hispanic, Asian and African American populations and there are a plethora of synagogues and churches representing many faiths and denominations. A cornucopia of upscale shops, designer boutiques and salons sweeps Middle Neck Road, the main thoroughfare. From kosher to Thai, Chinese and

Middle Eastern restaurants to European-style cafes with delectable desserts, a panorama of restaurants and eateries satiates every need.

For the young, parks filled with brightly-colored playgrounds and progressive pre-school programs energize the imagination. For seniors, the multipurpose Great Neck Senior Citizen Center on Grace Avenue offers a wide range of activities. Through the Great Neck Park District, residents of six villages and some unincorporated areas can also enjoy the Parkwood Sports Complex, including an Olympic-size swimming pool and children's pools, indoor and outdoor tennis courts and an indoor skating rink. Other villages offer private pool and athletic facilities to their residents, including a golf course in Lake Success. Great Neck has hiking trails, marinas and picnic areas. With Manhasset Bay to its east, the Long Island Sound at its tip and Little Neck Bay to the west, residents and visitors savor striking waterfront vistas

The world-class hospitals of the North Shore Long Island Jewish Health System and St. Francis Hospital, part of Catholic Health Services, are nearby.

Housing ranges from apartments, co-ops and condominiums to single-family homes and magnificent multi-acre estates. New assisted-living and independent-living facilities like The Atria and The Mayfair have opened in the past few years, in addition to the long-standing Grace Plaza of Great Neck, a nursing home. Visitors find luxurious accommodations at two hotels, the Inn at Great Neck and The Andrew.

Riding the Long Island Rail Road from the Great Neck station, which is part of the Port Washington branch to the city, takes from 25 to 30 minutes. There is commuter parking for residents. With frequent express service, it's the best commute of any line.

With so much to offer in its 9.6 square miles, Great Neck's unique character has always attracted movers and shakers, leaders in industry, health care, education and the arts, activists and philanthropists, hardworking and hard playing people who make a difference in all our lives, at home and beyond.

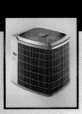    

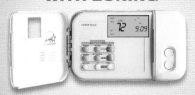

Wild Ginger

Pan Asian Cuisine

Wild Ginger has been a stunning success, elevating Pan-Asian food to new heights and producing taste sensations the likes of which had seldom been savored this side of the Pacific.

48 Great Neck Road, Great Neck

516.487.8288

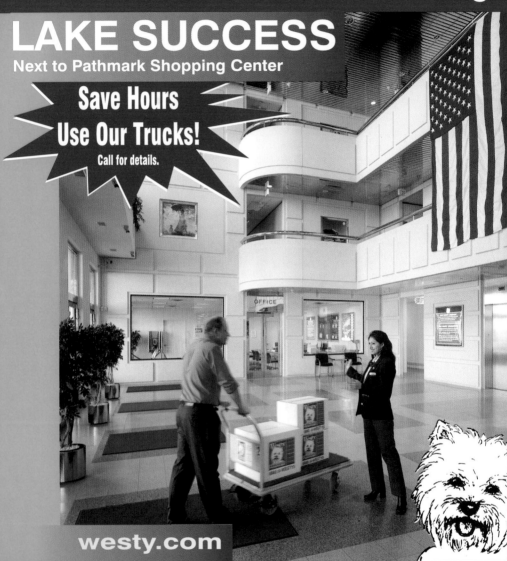

VACHERON CONSTANTIN

Manufacture Horlogère. Genève, depuis 1755.

Royal Eagle Day/Date

Métiers d'Art

Masterpieces. From time's finest artists.

JEWELS BY
VIGGI LTD.

FINE JEWELRY AND WATCHES

65 MIDDLE NECK ROAD • GREAT NECK, NY 11021 • TEL: 516.829.6161 • FAX: 516.466.8110

The Preservation of a Great Neck Landmark

*C*onveniently situated in the Village of Great Neck Plaza, this four-story iron and brick building known as the Thomaston Building is listed in the National Register of Historic Places. The building is a true reflection of the grace and charm of "Roaring 20's" architecture.

The Thomaston building, also known as 8 Bond Street, was commissioned by businessman W.R. Grace and designed by award-winning New York City architect James W. O'Conner in 1926.

The building was originally the corporate headquarters for the Grace Company's real estate operations. At one time, it was also the village hall.

Patrick Silberstein, the owner of the building, has made sure the beautiful old brick building with decorative wrought iron balconies is preserved for posterity. Silberstein also retro-fitted the interior of the building with old world charm. With its tall windows, graceful moldings and a stylish brick facade, the Thomaston Building ensures that history lives on.

THE THOMASTON BUILDING

BUSINESS OR PLEASURE AT THE INN

EXPECT TO EXCEED YOUR EXPECTATIONS

UNCOMPROMISING ACCOMMODATIONS · FIRST CLASS SERVICE · EXQUISITE AMBIANCE

INN AT GREAT NECK

Small Luxury Hotel

30 Cutter Mill Road . Great Neck . New York
www.innatgreatneck.com

CONCIERGE · BANQUET FACILITIES · CONFERENCE ROOMS · BUSINESS CENTER
HI-SPEED INTERNET ACCESS · IN ROOM SERVICE · EXERCISE ROOM · VALET PARKING

For Information And Reservations Call 516.773.2000

the
Giraffe room
lounge & restaurant

"In a classy little hotel. Signature food and atmosphere. Outstanding!" **Zagat 2001**

"The service excelled and the herb-roasted prime rib of beef was remarkable." **Newsday 2001**

HOTEL · RESTAURANT · CATERING · LOUNGE

Great Neck Garage & Repair Company - ca. 1906

Theodore DeBry Woodcut

THE NATIVES

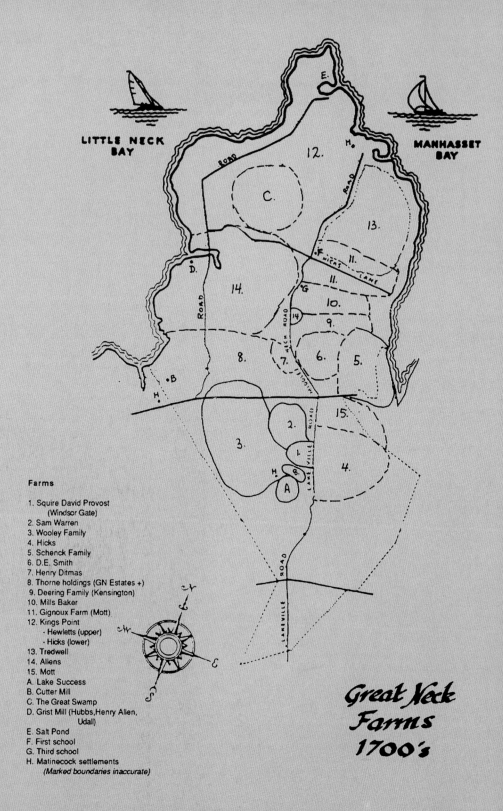

LITTLE NECK BAY

MANHASSET BAY

Farms

1. Squire David Provost
   (Windsor Gate)
2. Sam Warren
3. Wooley Family
4. Hicks
5. Schenck Family
6. D.E. Smith
7. Henry Ditmas
8. Thorne holdings (GN Estates +)
9. Deering Family (Kensington)
10. Mills Baker
11. Gignoux Farm (Mott)
12. Kings Point
    - Hewletts (upper)
    - Hicks (lower)
13. Tredwell
14. Aliens
15. Mott
A. Lake Success
B. Cutter Mill
C. The Great Swamp
D. Grist Mill (Hubbs, Henry Allen,
   Udall)
E. Salt Pond
F. First school
G. Third school
H. Matinecock settlements
   (Marked boundaries inaccurate)

Great Neck
Farms
1700's

Menhaden Ock

Before the Dutch and English settled the Great Neck peninsula in the mid-1600's, before the first town meeting in 1681, before the heat of revolution, there were natives.

The Mattinecock Indians (Mattinecock meaning high place) occupied the peninsula's shoreline, using the water for trade and fishing. They found their bounty in the Sound's oysters, crabs, clams, sturgeon, bass, and other fish. They grew buckwheat, cabbage, corn, flax, hay, oats, rutabaga, rye, and wheat. The natives hunted beaver, fox, quail, raccoon, weasel, and woodchuck.

The Mattinecock, like all the other natives, arrived via land bridge from Asia, and eventually made their way from Alaska to Great Neck. The peninsula's first residents were a branch of the Algonquin tribe and spoke the Algonquin language. They had plenty of family nearby: 13 Algonquin subtribes or small family clans scattered across Long Island

Anne Heatherton

From an old print

from Canarsie to Montauk. Each had a sachem, or chief, and occupied its own territory, bordered by trails, streams or clearly marked with stones. Neighboring tribes didn't cross territorial limits, or hunt or fish on each other's land.

Great Neck's natives were known as builders of grand canoes, 80 feet long and carved from the trunks of majestic trees. They also carved logs into totems for worship. Religion, it seems, was important on the peninsula from the start.

The natives lived together in long, low dwellings with several families occupying the same house. Each built its own fire in the middle of the bare earth floor to cook its food. The smoke escaped through a half-foot wide cut in the roof. The bark of chestnut trees and reeds were used to

(from an old print.)

"Mad Nan holds her own."

A fiery female called "Mad" Nan lived here three centuries ago. Today she is a lost lady of history, but she inspired the name of the town.

form the sides and roof. The natives used wooden dippers for drinking water, kept maize and beans in small baskets and stored their collections of earthen pots, clay bowls and spoons fashioned from dry gourd shells close to the hearth.

The natives on Long Island were wealthier than most, and spent much of their time gambling, playing ball, and games that improved their warrior skills with a bow and arrow. When the settlers came, the indians often drank to excess.

Like Great Neckers today, the natives also celebrated important moments in their lives with a splash. They partied at harvest time and held baby-naming ceremonies that included shouting the name of the baby three times, followed by dancing, eating and lavishing the newborn with gifts. Long before Great Neck's first Bar or Bat Mitzvah, natives reaching adolescence celebrated their rite-of-passage by hunting alone in the woods. A girl's coming-of-age was marked by cutting off her hair and being cloistered for several days in a designated wigwam in the village. Even weddings, in these days before catering halls, were an occasion to remember. To marry off their sons, fathers tried to make a good impression on their prospective in-laws, bestowing animal gifts to the parents of eligible girls in the village. When it was a match, the prospective bride's parents accepted their offerings. History, however, did not record who paid for the wedding.

The natives referred to what we now know Great Neck as Menhaden-Ock, most likely because of the amount of fish. The name would eventually, with the arrival of European settlers (English) in the 1640's, evolve into Madnan's Neck, then Great Madnan's Neck, and then, by 1670, Great Neck. The last reference to Madnan's Neck appeared in 1752. Reference to Great Neck as Mathew Garreson's Neck has also been found.

An alternate explanation of the name "Madnan's Neck" is offered by most historians: Anne (or Nan) Hutchinson (or Heatherton), a haughty Englishwoman tried to take over (what is now) Kings Point upon arrival. Though she seemed to have a knack for location, and may have had one of the first thriving real estate businesses in these parts, she could never procure a grant or a clear title to the land she desired. Her temper earned her the nickname Mad Nan, and from there comes the name. This is, however, merely folklore. (It is interesting to note, though, that Anne Hutchinson (of Boston fame) did, in fact, perish at the hands of natives on Long Island in 1643.

At first, the settlers and natives coexisted well, with the settlers offering their technology in exchange for the natives' know-how. The settlers even began working

The Lakeville AME Zion Church, ca. 1833

with wampum, the Indian currency made of shells. Soon, however, the relationship began to deteriorate. Charges of unfriendly native behavior became common among settlers; they claimed that the natives hurt their cattle and damaged their homes, and that the Indians' dogs were ferocious nuisances.

In fact, on November 18, 1659, a law was imposed forcing compensation for white property damaged by natives. Later, both Director-General of New Netherlands William Kieft and his successor, Peter Stuyvesant, tried their respective hands at solving the growing problem, but to no avail. (New Netherlands area was roughly present day New York State.)

The natives, led by Tackapousha, claimed that the produce of the land and not the land itself had been sold. They disputed the November 18, 1643 sale of the Hempstead Plains, which included the Great Neck peninsula, to the Reverend Robert Fordham and John Carman. In 1657, 1666, and 1677, settlers (including local magistrates Richard Gildersleeve and John Seaman, along with John Hicks and William Yeats) testified in court to having seen the transaction take place. Tackapousha was not appeased, and in 1684, with the issue still pressing, a commission of settlers was elected to solve the problem, and was granted license to pay off the natives. (Tackapousha had requested 120 pounds sterling.)

Intermarriage was prevalent among the natives, and by the turn of the 17th century, there most likely were no natives of pure lineage left. They married into both the white and slave populations. As a result of smallpox, the general native population dwindled throughout the end of the century. Most of those that remained ended up grouping together on what is now Community Drive. There are numerous natives, Tackapousha included, buried in the Zion AME Church's cemetery on

Early English illustration by John White called The Manner of Their Fishing---depicting Native Americans along the Atlantic seaboard.

Community Drive in what is now part of Manhasset.

The Lakeville AME Zion Church was founded by freed slaves and Mattinecock settlers of the Sucat Pond or Suckess community, as the area was known in 1833, five years after slavery was abolished in New York. Originally called the colored people's meeting house, it is one of the oldest black churches in New York State. Not welcome elsewhere in those days, Indians and African Americans worshipped at the church built on a winding dirt path across from where North Shore University Hospital now stands. A simple wooden cross sits atop the gable on the white frame church. Stones and crosses are strewn across the cemetery, part of which was recently restored. Efforts are also underway to preserve the historic edifice.

Long Island Indians befriended the early European settlers, as depicted in this idealized mural of the Hempstead settlement painted by Peppino Mangravite in 1937. Courtesy, National Archives.

THE SETTLERS

Madnan's Neck

The first European to set eyes upon the Long Island peninsula was the Captain Adrian Block of the Great Dutch West India Company in 1614, four years after Henry Hudson made his trip west. The Dutch attorney's third trip to the West nearly ended in disaster when his ship, "The Tiger," burned and sank shortly following its landing. He and his men, camping at the southern tip of Manhattan Island, sat stupefied as their only way home, crammed with valuable animal pelts and wampum went down in flames.

Exhibiting true New York spirit, the Captain and his men built a ship over a New York winter. His new ship, "The Restless," was fashioned out of timber and the few nails they managed to salvage from their charred vessel. When the sailors set sail again, they did so in the direction of Long Island. Block sailed around the Island, mapping it as he passed. A near catastrophe had led to discovery.

The Reverend Robert Fordham and his brother-in-law, John Carman, came to Hempstead via the Long Island Sound from New Haven and proceeded to scout the area. The law in New Haven stipulated that enfranchisement was tied to one's church. This was unacceptable to most residents, so the community sent Fordham and Carman to negotiate a deal for land.

The deal with Chief Tackapousha occurred during this trip, and on November 16 of the following year, William Kieft granted a special patent for the territory, along with permission for the community's incorporation. The people of Hempstead (or, as the Dutch called it, Hemestede) had the right to religious self-determination.

Kieft granted those rights on the condition that the settlers use the Dutch system of weights and measurements and pay a tax of one tenth of their produce ten years after the first general peace with the Indians was established. The political independence of the new community was so extensive that the only town officials who were in any way elected by the Dutch government were the magistrates, who were first nominated

Peter Stuyvesant's moment of decision. Courtesy - The Long Island Story by Alexander M. Swaab

by a town meeting.

Most of the Stamford community, led in part by the Reverend Richard Denton, followed their scouts to their new home. Hempstead, which included what is presently a majority of Nassau County, had been settled.

The Dutch ruled Long Island from 1642 to 1664 or so, and 1673 to 1674. Under Dutch rule, town meetings elected overseers, constables and local officers, and nominated magistrates, and passed legislation.

Peter Stuyvesant named the first two magistrates of Hempstead, John Seaman and Richard Gildersleeve, on December 21, 1656. The two could not have been more incompatible.

Seaman, a half Quaker of noted lineage, was known as a genial man. During the resurgence of Dutch authority on Long Island from 1673 to 1674, he was dubbed *schepen*, a term of honor akin to the English's knighting. Gildersleeve, a self-made man of English descent, was noted for his hatred of Quakers. Once, he jailed a Quaker preacher in his house (there was no jail), then sent him off to New York by foot and had him tied to a wheelbarrow with a slave and lashed until the preacher began to work. He was also strongly anti-Dutch, and at the forefront of a pro-English push in the early 1660's. He served as townsman for the first time in 1664 and still played the town's drum at age 82.

Samuel Allen and George Hewlett watched the town's cattle. Allen, one of 40 original Madnan's Neck Allens, claimed to trace his lineage back to Pyrus Allen, Lord Mayor of London in 1247. One of George Hewlett's descendants would later live at the tip of what is now Kings Point, hence the one-time appellation Hewlett's Point. Hewlett also maintained the town gate.

Adam Mott was the town drummer for some time. Captain John Scott served as Town Agent, and Thomas Hicks, John Hicks' son, was Town Clerk. Later, English Governor Edmond Andros appointed Thomas Hicks the first judge on the county court.

Madnan's Neck had an extremely proactive local government. A tax on liquor was imposed. Half the tax paid for the town's supply of ammunition; the other half for education.

The "Lawes of God," established on September 16, 1650 at a meeting of the General court, and consented to on October 18 of that year by a town meeting, provided a regious code of ethics, including conduct on holidays, for the whole town. Punishments for poor conduct included fines, corporal punishment, and banishment.

A charge of such misconduct was filed, anonymously, on October 3, 1659, against Henry Linnington. His was the first recorded solicitation for sexual favors in the peninsula's history. Linnington was threatened with banishment, but promised to reform his behavior and was allowed to stay.

OTHER EARLY GREAT NECK FIRSTS

First house of worship in Hempstead: Erected in 1645, its floor was 24 sq. ft.

First child born in Hempstead: Caleb Carman was born August 6, 1639 to John and Florence Carman.

First inn in Hempstead: The inn was licensed in 1659.

First transaction in Madnan's Neck: Richard Gildersleeve and Adam Mott traded land in 1670.

First grist mill: Built by Thomas Rushmore in 1679 with the permission of Governor Andros.

First Madnan's Neck town meeting and town vote: February 10, 1681, Neckers vote to continue to support the Hempstead government and pay their proportionate share of the Town Hall's maintenance.

The First Fight

It was around this time that Madnan's Neck began to separate from Hempstead. As its population grew, independence from Hempstead became more easily attained.

In the election for constable of Hempstead, 1672, Robert Jackson, a prominent resident of Madnan's Neck, beat out Simon Seryon (or Searing), 39-31. Seryon, however, was declared the winner. Outraged Madnan's Neckers petitioned the Governor for a separation, but their request was denied.

Madnan's Neckers were not satisfied with the service they were receiving from their minister, and in February, 1661, Director-General Stuyvesant received a letter complaining that for want of a preacher, children were going unbaptized. One month later, the Reverend Samuel Drisius arrived and baptized 41 children and an old woman. The residents of Madnan's Neck continued without a preacher of their own for years.

On May 6, 1682, a majority vote at a town meeting in Hempstead declared the Reverend Jeremy Hobart the minister. But Hobart neglected his duty to service Madnan's Neck. This is evidenced by Christopher Yeamans' complaints that Hempstead was too far away to travel to on Sundays and that Hobart had come to Madnan's Neck's church once in three years. The Governor ordered the Reverend to visit Madnan's Neck at least once a month.

Edward Hare, in a letter to the Governor, complained that when Hobart took his now monthly visit to the peninsula, he did so during the week, when people were too busy working to see him. He declared that Madnan's Neck had gone too long without a proper minister, and had hired the Reverend Morgan Jones in June of 1682. (The years (or year, that is, 1682) hint at an error in either the Hempstead records or Hare's argument.)

Either way, Hobart responded to the letter early in 1687 by forcing Jones to leave Madnan's Neck and demanding four years back pay. The residents of Madnan's Neck refused to pay for services they had not received, and requested a religious school for their children, numbering roughly 60. The Governor sent a copy of Madnan's Neck's petition for a religious school and proper minister to Hobart on May 31, 1687, requesting that Hobart, "show cause, on Monday next, why he don't preach there."

Finally, on June 9, 1687, Madnan's Neck was ordered to pay Hobart his four years' pay, the Reverend Morgan Jones was officially made Madnan's Neck's minister, and it was ordered that Madnan's Neck be "separate hereafter from Hempstead." The town was given its own constable and marshal. Edward Hare, who had helped move Madnan's Neck's quest for independence along, filled the post of constable. The separation, though only a religious one, was very important. Madnan's Neck would gain more control over itself with time.

The pre-Revolutionary years were marked by even less dependence on Hempstead. Few communities of Madnan's Neck's size — 61 landowners as of March, 1658, over 100 by 1700 — had its own constable, marshal, church, minister, grist mill, pound, and highway and fence repairman.

The Saddle Rock Grist Mill

One of Great Neck's historical jewels, the Saddle Rock Grist Mill, sits just inside a cove leading into Little Neck Bay. It was built before the turn of the 17th century and has been restored to ca. 1845 and is now listed in the Federal Historical Landmark Registry. At the time of construction, the area was primarily agricultural, and the mill was highly profitable.

Henry Allen bought the mill from Richard Hubbs, Jr. on February 18, 1702. Allen received permission to operate the mill on the condition that if he ever decided to stop running the mill, he would turn control of the mill over to the town. He was also instructed to keep the mill in good repair and informed that he should only "grind for the Town for the twelfth part," i.e., he was allowed to charge those who used his mill up to one twelfth of what he ground.

Allen never decided to give it up, however, and the mill remained within his family until 1829. The mill was passed from Henry to his son John, who in 1785 passed the mill on to his oldest son, David. After David Allen's death in 1829, ownership of the mill turned up in the hands of John Tredwell. A few years later, Richard Udall bought the mill, and it remained in his family's hands for over 120 years until it was donated to the Nassau County Historical Society in 1950.

In the 19th century the mill was not only a place to grind flour, but also barley, bran, buckwheat, chicken feed, corn, graham, Indian meal, middlings, oats, and rye. The Udalls built a dock next to the mill and shipped to New York what they and their customers produced. The sloops returned from the big city with manufactured goods and manure, shoveled off the New York streets, to be used by the farmers as fertilizer.

As the great milling centers of the Midwest opened, the Saddle Rock Grist Mill became obsolete and fell into disrepair. Mrs. Louise Udall Eldridge, who was elected the mayor of the Village of Saddle Rock after its incorporation and was the first female mayor in New York State, restored the mill to working condition in 1940, adding electric motors to the 200-year old structure.

The New York Herald Tribune reported on February 5, 1940 that the mill had been restored and would resume grinding that week. Today, the Saddle Rock Grist Mill is the oldest operating tidal grist mill in the country.

Henry Allen's Grist Mill---Later to become The Saddle Rock Grist Mill

HENRY ALLEN

THE MAN
who once
owned...

GREAT NECK

A Search Through Musty Court Records
Reveals The Success Story of
Our Community's First Land Baron.

It was in the year 1711 when an influential resident of Great Neck, one Henry Allen, was chosen "Keeper of the Gates & Fences." This was a top-flight job in those days. Allen's duties consisted of hanging gates on various thoroughfares to keep cattle from straying into the Village. But history remembers Henry Allen not so much for his cattle-corralling chores as for his land-grabbing acumen.

Unquestionably, Henry Allen was the shrewdest real estate operator ever seen in these parts with the exception of the gentle-man who bought Manhattan from the Indians for $24.00. Henry Allen gobbled up Great Neck's juiciest acreage long before the phrase "land-boom" was ever coined. His brother was equally astute, too, as a search through Great Neck property transfers of a few centuries ago reveals. Here with documentary quoted from Ye Olde Towne Records:

March 31, 1664 Sam'l Allen is to keep the west herd of cows at Madnan's Neck.

Oct. 2, 1664 Sam'l Allen buys a piece of land from Jos. Genens.

Oct. 11, 1666 Sam'l Allen buys land in Madnan's Neck from, John Willy (Wooley)

Dec. 22, 1668 Sam'l Allen has a law suit. (Oh, ho!, Sam! Watch your step and Merry Xmas!)

This is the last we hear of this first recorded Allen, however, as from now on "Henery" (so spelled in old records) heads the house. And was he a top-notch trader!

Jan. 8, 1692 Henry Allen buys from his brother Samuel a piece of land on Madnan's Neck

Dec. 22, 1698 Henry Allen buys land on Madnan's Neck, from Richard Thorne

build a grist mill.

Note: Three generations of Allens ran this mill – In fact, it was known as Allen's Mill until the Udall's came to town in 1935.

However, for some reason we have been unable to unearth, the mill was not erected until 1710. "Henery" went right on buying right and left, living graciously in a delightful house near where the old mill now stands at our favorite skating pond in Saddle Rock. Here's more evidence of his ever mounting perspicacity:

June 12, 1700 Henry Allen gets more land near his own.

April 21, 1705 Henry Allen buys land from David Jeycocks.

May 3, 1705 Henry Allen buys land from Thomas Rushmore.

April 1, 1706 Henry Allen buys 15acres from Richard and Thomas Ellison in Madnan's.

May 11, 1706 Henry Allen buys 21acres from John Comes for 40 pounds on the neck.

April 1, 1708 At a town meeting Henry Allen was chosen surveyor of the highways and fence viewre.

Ah! there, Henery. You certainly knew sterling real estate when you viewed it – and wasn't April fools your lucky day? (We didn't notice any of your many transactions recorded on a Friday the 13th, however.) But here's a tip off on what H. A. thought of our neighboring neck to the northeast.

Apr. 1, 1709 Henry Allen SELLS (Note: he SELLS!) land at head of Cow Neck to Jno. Rushmore.

Feb. 22, 1710 Henry Allen BUYS 46 acres of land on Madnan's Neck

from John Rushmore. "Some swap," hey!

Jan. 23, 1710 Sales of several pieces of land to Henry Allen on Madnan's Neck confirmed.

Apr. 4, 1710 Henry Allen buys from John Carman 10 acres on North Side for 8 pounds.

Apr. 4, 1710 Henry Allen buys from Thomas Gildersleeve two 10 acre plots for 20 pounds.

May 9, 1711 Henry Allen buys from Able Smith 33 acres on Madnan's Neck for 4 pounds.

May 22, 1711 Henry Allen buys from Rob't Hubbs 51 acres on Madnan's Neck for 300 pounds.

Hum! Quite a difference in price in those last two. Land must have boomed overnight.

May 6, 1713 released to Henry Allen by Thomas Hicks, John Jackson an John Treadwell, Town Trustees 24 acres on Madnan's Neck.

And that apparently was the last deal of King Henry, the 1st of Madnan's – but he did hand down his crown and sceptre in truly regal fashion to his son – another right royal real estater: Carry on!

Apr. 16, 1733 Henry Allen No. 2 and Phoebe (Williams) his wife sell out their rights of inheritance to the estate of the late Henry No. 1 for the sum of 1000 pounds.

But notice on the very same date this other entry in Ye Olde Towne Records:

Apr. 16, 1733 Henry Allen No. 2 buys 270 acres of land from Abel Smith and Deborah, his wf. on Madnan's Neck for 1650 pounds. Bounded on the N. by Geo. Hewlett and Daniel Kissam, East by Hewlett, Jos. Williams and Rob't Mitchell. South by Allens. West by the Bay.

This Henry No. 2 sure started off with a bang! And now just watch his dust!

Nov. 2, 1738 Henry Allen No. 2 is serving as Justice of the peace.

Apr. 6, 1742 Henry Allen No.2 is chosen as one of the Surveyors of Highways.

Jul. 11, 1745 John and Philip Allen buy 157 acres on East side of GREAT NECK, for 1507 pounds; from Adam Mott in 3 parts.

Mr. Mott seems to have been divided like "All Gaul."

And what happened to our original Henry Allen? Here, now, is a classic document that we transcribe from old, yellowed recordings of the last wills and testaments of our most illustrious fellow townsmen back there in the dim past "when men were men" and widows wept.

Under the date of: "March, anno Dom. 1726. we reverently quote you this:

"I, Henry Allyne of Madnan's's Neck, being in bodily health, I leave to my wife Mary 1/3 of my movable estate. AND THE USE OF THE BEST ROOM IN MY HOUSE and the use of 1/3 of my home farm or plantation. I leave to the poor of Queen's County 50 pounds to be distributed among the poor and needy at the discretion of my executors. I leave all my lands and meadows to all my sons, BUT with no power to SELL until they are 30 years old.

Wise old Henry!...and also note this splendid spirit of conversation:

"And they are to cut no timber except as necessity requires. The rest of my personal estate I leave to my daughters, and they are to live in my house till they are married. (Names are not given) I make Theodoras Van Wyck Esq. George Hewlett and William Mott, all of Madnan's Neck, my executors."

This precious document was proved on August 19, 1728 and the witnesses were: William Burch, Richbell Mott and Henry Underwood. And then, tragically, in a brief testament dated June 22, 1747 we come upon this note of anticlimax:

"I, Mary Allen, widow of Henry Allen of Great Neck, being far advanced in years do leave to my eldest son Henry the sum of 5 pounds." - - -

And mentions other bequests: to John and Philip, eldest daughter Mary, Hannah, wife of John Wooley, Alice, wife of John Clap, Sarah, wife of Benj. Tredwell, Elizabeth, wife of Wm. Mott and Phebe, wife of Thomas Smith. And that's that!

The Battle of Long Island - "Retreat of the Americans under Gen. Stiling across Gowanus Creek," Jentered according to act of Congress A.D. 1877 by Johnson & Miles in the office of the Librarian of Congress at Washington.

INDEPENDENCE

Independence

As revolution came closer to Madnan's Neck, hereafter referred to as Great Neck, the quiet agricultural town worked itself into a frenzy.

Devoutly patriotic, the farmers of the peninsula teamed up with their contemporaries in Cow Neck (now Port Washington), and readied themselves for the fight of a lifetime.

Many residents of the two peninsulas declared themselves the "Committee for the District of Cow Neck and Great Neck & C." Their purpose, as stipulated by a document known as the "Form of Association," was to engage in a "vigorous prosecution of the measures necessary for [America's] safety… for the purpose of preserving our constitution and opposing the execution of the several arbitrary and oppressive acts of the British Parliament, until a reconciliation between Great Britain and America, on constitution principles… can be obtained…" They did so in the wake of "the bloody scene… in Massachusetts Bay" and new taxes.

On October 4, 1775, the committee declared that it would be best for the residents of the two necks to separate from Hempstead, whose behavior was considered "inimical to freedom." "[T]herefore," the declaration continued, "in all matters relative to the Congressional plan, we shall consider ourselves as an entire, separate and independent beat or district."

The Provincial Congress of New York responded that they "highly approve" eight days later. In 1784, the split became official, as Benjamin Ackley managed to push the creation of the Town of North Hempstead through all necessary channels.

Early in 1776, the committee voted to bar Tories (those who aligned themselves politically with England) from moving to the Cow Neck and Great Neck areas. The new Whig party, supporting the Continental Congress and independance, had prevailed.

Though no major battles took place in Great Neck and the Battle of Long Island came near, but not into, Northern Hempstead, the peninsula was a very dangerous place to live during the American Revolution. Riots, mob gatherings, plundering, and robbery were common, and directed at neither the Tories nor Whigs; rather, the molestation was indiscriminately carried out. The Allen Mill (Today's Saddle Rock Grist Mill) was robbed numerous times during the revolution. It was at this time that women began carrying small pistols, known as "muff-pistols," in their muffs whenever they left the house.

As part of General George Washington's North Shore Spy Ring, Great Neckers fielded intelligence reports. Some local soldiers were sent on horseback to the south shore to patrol the Rockaway Coast. Others crossed the Long Island Sound to attack British forts in Connecticut.

Because of Great Neck's proximity to the Sound and New York, both the Continental Army and the British forces were intent on controlling the region. In 1776, William Hicks was ordered by the Continental Army to take his men to the tip of Kings Point (then Hewlett's Point) and watch the Sound for the British. He was to report any ship movements to Major Richard Thorne, commander of the Great Neck Mulitia. Some historians had theorized that Hicks and his men neglected their duties. Orders were received a month later that the men were not to play cards, drink, or waste ammunition shooting game.

When the British took control after the Battle of Long Island, The English army, serving under General Howe, demanded needed supplies from Great Neck's residents. They plundered Great Neck's fields. Pirates known as "whaleboaters" also took advantage of the chaos. They stole and killed seemingly at will, and then retreated to their bases on the Connecticut shore.

The revolution left Great Neck in disrepair. The small agricultural town would rebound, however, and soon change dramatically. The new century would bring a new face to Great Neck, one of prosperity and cosmopolitanism never before seen on Long Island.

At a town meeting in Hempstead, Northern Hempstead and the rest of Hempstead officially split on April 6, 1784. The statement separating the towns declared that each town would elect its own town officers and care for the poor within its borders.

The first official North Hempstead meeting took place the next day. Colonel John Sands and Richard Valentine, Esq. were placed in charge of the details involved in separation. In time, more offices would be established, such as the Overseer of the Poor, Appraiser of "Intestates Estates," and other titles.

North Hempstead's first Supervisor, Adrian Onderdonk of Sands Point was elected. His grandson, Henry Onderdonk later became one of the foremost authorities on Long Island's early history. And so, North Hempstead was born.

"Muff pistols" were carried as a deterrent by women. This amazing little pistol had a concealed trigger that was revealed when the hammer is cocked making the pistol easy to draw and fire.

Whaleboats were used by pirates who plundered Great Neck's shores after the British took control.
published by Ch. Magnus 12 Frankfort St. NY

Schenck Bros. Carriage Makers - Middle Neck Road - ca. 1886

THE 1800's

SCHENCK BROS.
CARRIAGE MAKERS.

The 1800's:
Welcoming Affluence

"Success comes to a writer, as a rule, so gradually that it is always something of a shock to him to come back and realize the heights to which he has climbed." - *P.G. Wodehouse*

The turn of the century was quiet as the post-war rebuilding process began. Farms were reconstructed, fields reapportioned, families relocated.

The start of the 19th century marked the beginning of a new Great Neck. Soon, many of the wealthiest New Yorkers would buy summer homes in Great Neck. The summer homes, with the advent of the train and car, later became suburban year-round homes. And then, years after the process began, the well-to-do, well-educated, proactive suburbanites of this Gold Coast suburb made Great Neck into a self-serving community.

Crampton Brothers Livery

The Great Neck Train Station, early 1800's

Getting There:
The Railroad & The Ferry

Before the Long Island Railroad began shuttling Great Neckers to and from New York by the thousands, there was a ferry. First established not for commuters, but for trade, ferry service peaked in the early to mid 1800's. The ferries landed on Hewlett's Dock, Woolley's Dock, and later, near the grist mill landing.

It was at this time that the old Allen Mill became the old Udall Mill, and with the change in ownership came a change in operations. The Udalls rented space on their dock to others. Vigorous trade with the city ensued. In 1850 the Udalls built their own sloop, "The Richard Udall," and sent it to the city stocked with hay and other items, including apples, eggs, lumber, pears, pork, potatoes, tomatoes, turnips, and flour ground at the mill for the urban consumers.

The ferries and sloops, sent to New York full, did not return to the peninsula empty. The return trip often brought manufactured goods, such as hardware and farm tools, to Great Neck, along with items such as sugar, rice and coffee.

The chief trade, however, involved hay and manure. Starting in the 1820's, Great Neck farmers began to grow their own hay after a dispute with their business partners in Hempstead left them without access to the abundance of hay in Hempstead. The Great Neckers proceeded to sell their hay to New York, which in those days moved in horse-drawn carriages. On the way back, the sloops would be filled with manure from the very horses the incoming trips were feeding to fertilize the lush, rolling hills of agricultural Great Neck.

Two prominent citizens, Whitehead Hewlett and James Udall, founded the Great Neck Steamboat Wharf Company. By 1834, the steamboats "The Sun" and "The Statesman" provided transportation to the city for commuters. The trip to New York from the Grist Mill took two hours.

The large ferry "Sewanaka," most popular during the summer, left Great Neck enroute to New York, landing at 31st Street and Peck's Slip, near Wall Street at 7 a.m. daily. The return trip began at 4 p.m. The ferry, a steamboat, was utilized by some of Great Neck's most well known citizens, and when it burned on its way back to the peninsula in June of 1880, the community grieved. It was soon replaced by the "Idlewild," which, like a yacht, had staterooms rented by the season by regulars like William R. Grace. The Idlewild remained in service for a long time.

The trip originated in Sea Cliff, with stops at Glen Cove, Sands Point, and Great Neck. The Great Neck stop was at the end of Steamboat Road, which at the time continued through the Merchant Marine Academy. The fare was 50 cents per per-

son, and the entire community from farmers to Wall Street tycoons used the service.

people," Childs wrote. "One lady remarked we were like a dog show made up of different specimens. Perhaps because there were so many kinds of people it made Society all the more delightful.....Life at Great Neck was much like the English country life of the novels of those days. Large house parties, much entertaining of all sorts, also much formality. We all dressed for dinner, the men in evening clothes, as the Englishman does to this day and as the American still does sometimes, and always should. .... We danced much - waltzes, lanciers, Virginia reels. What is more, we had been carefully taught to dance. Occasionally, there would be a barn dance. The stables were large and handsomely fin-

---

Life at Great Neck was much like the English country life of the novels of those days. - Emily Robbins Child

---

Upon arrival at home, an assemblage of carriages and opulently clad wives greeted their husbands after a long day's work. Some of the younger women drove their own dog carts, their grooms outfitted in coats studded with silver buttons, white breeches, boots and a silk hat, despite the warm weather.

Emily Robbins Childs recalled her trip to Great Neck on the Idlewild in an essay, "The Newport of the Sound," that appeared in The Book of Great Neck in 1936. She recalled staying at the Hewlett place for the summer, one of about 30 estates at the time. The village, she said, included a post office, two or three general stores, blacksmiths, a few houses and a small meat market. Most summer residents went to Manhattan for their meat. "We found Great Neck had many delightful

ished and made a good background for decorations of all sorts - flags, bunting and flowers, etc....There was a new dance called "dancing in the barn" which some of us taught the others, and rather scandalized the chaperones."

Back then, social positions were taken seriously. Properly gowned, society sallied forth, calling cards in hand, for endless rounds of calling and receiving calls. Once a year, visits had to be exchanged with everyone on the calling lists.

The pamphlet entitled *Old Great Neck: A Stroll in Memories' Lane* relates a story about William R. Grace and his friend, James E. Ward. "The two men met at the landing by their drivers in light road wagons and a team of horses. Both Mr. Ward and Mr. Grace, upon getting into the wagon took the reins and the race was on. The roads were narrow and very dusty, their horses were fast and they both were good drivers and good sports as well as good friends." Such was the atmosphere in Great Neck.

In 1866, the North Shore Railroad Company, financed by several key Great Neckers, built an extension of the New York and Flushing Railroad to their hometown. The tracks' westernmost point was Long Island City, where city commuters took the ferry. A

"It seems to me there was no one in Great Neck too poor to own a horse and buggy. And everyone simply had to have a sleigh."
- Emily Robbins Child

It was during the ferry era that Great Neck's use as a summer resort reached its climax. Hotels sprouted up on Steamboat Road and Middle Neck Road, and fishing was common further south in Lake Success.

Because of the lack of produce to be sold in the winter, along with concern that the ferry and its passengers could not last through the harsh weather of a New York winter, water transportation ran only during the summer. This forced the wealthy New York City businessmen away from their fantastic mansions and easygoing, rural home life for the winter months, and sent them back to Manhattan.

And so they traveled back every fall, leaving what they knew would be a beautiful winter of gentle hills blanketed in vanilla-white snow followed by a magnificent, multi-colored thaw. Instead, they traversed the well-fertilized, noisy, slush-filled streets of 19th century Manhattan until Great Neck found a way to commute to the city in the winter.

train tunnel from Long Island City into Manhattan was completed only in 1910.

Compared with steamboats, the train, was unpopular, and ownership of the extension changed hands three years later, when the North Shore (or North Side) Railroad system took over. Plagued by financial difficulty, the new owner folded over a decade later. The Long Island Railroad built its first station in Great Neck in 1883, and took control of the lines in 1884. The steam drawn railroad gained popularity.

As a result of the station's presence, the southern section of the commercial district, which to that point had consisted of little more than a couple of general stores, began to grow.

The LIRR updated its service with new stations and better connections to Manhattan in 1898. In that same year, the tracks were electrified and extended to Port Washington.

Grace Vacario and Jack, ca. 1800's - Kings Point

The Poet 'Lariet' of Great Neck

Cutter Mill Road, one of the major thoroughfares near the station, got its name from the prominent early 19th century landowner and gentleman farmer who owned the surrounding acreage: Bloodgood Haviland Cutter.

B orn in 1817 in an unincorporated area of Great Neck near Little Neck, Cutter collected curios and revolutionary relics. Though much of his knowledge came from the Bible and he had little formal education, Cutter grew rich holding farm mortgages and stock market investments. But it was for his fanciful poetry, often written on the spur of the moment, that Cutter was best known. A frequent traveler to Europe, it was on a five-month journey on the steamer Quaker City to the Holy Lands in 1867 that Cutter happened upon another scribe, Mark Twain. The two became friends.

In the notes for Twain's travel book *The Innocents Abroad*, Cutter was his "Poet Lariat." Twain described Cutter this way: "He is fifty years old, and small of his age. He dresses in homespun, and is a simple-minded, honest, old-fashioned farmer, with a strange proclivity for writing rhymes. He writes them on all possible subjects, and

gets them printed on slips of paper, with his portrait at the head. These he will give to any man who comes along, whether he has anything against him or not."

While he could never compare to the master wordsmith, in 1886, Cutter had his own 500-page collection of his poetry, "The Long Island Farmer's Poems," published by a vanity press.

When he was a boy, Cutter's mother, Mary Bloodgood, remarried . Young Cutter moved to Prospect Hill, a 102-acre farm owned by his grandfather, Roe Haviland. The elder gentleman, however, soon forced Cutter to leave school and earn his keep on one of his coastal schooners. Cutter worked his way to master of one of the ships. Then in 1840 he eloped with 16-year-old Emeline Allen, of the prominent Great Neck Allens. When Grandfather Haviland died four years later, Cutter inherited Prospect Hill. As a gentleman farmer he gave poetry readings and his verse was sometimes published in local papers.

With his old-fashioned clothes and country accent, Cutter was often sighted on the streets of Flushing reading from the open Bible in his hands. Though some reports called him an honest sort with a keen business sense, others claimed he was hypocritical and quick to foreclose mortgages on widows and orphans. Among his holdings were large blocks of land north of the railroad station and much of the village of Plandome Heights.

When Glen Cove celebrated its 200th anniversary in 1868, the poet William Cullen Bryant was asked to write a commemorative ode. He declined. Bloodgood Cutter, known as the "Long Island Farmer Poet," picked up the task and wrote these lines:

THE
LONG ISLAND FARMER
POET.

Excerpt from - The Bicentennial Celebration at Glen Cove, May 24, 1868.

My friends, we have assembled here,
To celebrate the two hundredth year.
Of this your pleasant dwelling-place,
And to thank our ancestral race,

For choosing this location grand,
As any in our common land;
Here you have a fine water view,
With all its privileges, too.

Oysters and clams grow on your shore,
You have them brought fresh to your door;
Then they are a delicious treat,
But canned, they're hardly fit to eat.

Last summer we had them on the ship,
While on our long excursion trip;
I did not fancy then their taste,
So quantities did go to waste.

Then, if you want salt water fish,
Can have the kind just as you wish;
Or if you want the splendid trout,
Go to your ponds and fish them out.

Here you have bathing-places good,
Where you can enjoy the briny flood;
In summer citizens here come,
To bathe and enjoy your rural home.

For bathing in the briny swell,
You know they generally pay well;
That is a great advantage too,
And benefits many of you.

With all these blessings at command,
You need not seek another land;
But here you should contented live,
And thanks to the Almighty give.

Two hundred years have passed away,
And as to our fathers, where are they?
Old Father Time has laid them low,
And with us all 'twill soon be so.

Nearly 3 months before he died, this article about Bloodgood Cutter appeared in the New York Herald.

July 1, 1906 - There lives in comparative obscurity, the most romantic, picturesque and original character in contemporary American life. There is a spiritual quality about the fine old face, an elemental nobility about his splendidly modeled head, thatched with silken white hair - his is the face of a poet - whatever the shortcomings of his metrical expression.

"Come along and see my collection." From basement to garret its great rooms are piled full to choking with art objects and curios, gathered in his travels by the "Poet Lariat" from every nook and corner of Europe and Asia. To enumerate all the wonderful things it contains would require many volumes of catalogs. They include everything from fantastic old French bedsteads, German clocks and Venetian glasses, to curiously wrought warming pans and swords of many periods.

"But I have managed to be powerful happy, even if I am only a plain Long Island farmer and while I stand for education every time I do think some people have too much, and too much education has a tendency to make men selfish and sometimes unkind."

Cutter died in September, 1906 at the age of 89. A tall granite headstone in the Zion Episcopal Church cemetery in Douglaston marks his burial site.

Bloodgood H. Cutter's Old Homestead, Little Neck, L.I.

They Used to Commute by
STEAMBOAT

If You're Tired of being a Standee on the L.I.R.R.,
Then Step Aboard the S.S. Idlewild for a Leisurely Cruise to Manhattan.
Here is Nostalgic Local History That Will make You Want to Tear Up Your Commutation Ticket.

by Richard Schisgall

At eight o'clock each morning a large paddlewheel boat bound for Manhattan left Great Neck from a dock at Steamboat Landing. At about six o'clock each evening a colorful array of equipages, filled with hand-some women dressed in the season's finery, lined the same dock to await the return of the ship. It was the big event of the day. Great Neck's gentlemen of commerce, with business establishments in New York City, were returning home from a day's work at the office.

Quite a contrast from the flurry of shiny new sedans and convertibles that crowds the Great Neck station each afternoon, as the 4:55 or 5:25 pulls in. For this was the year 1876, when the population of Great Neck numbered about 1,200 people. Middle Neck Road was a dirt path at the time, lined with two general stores owned by the Hayden brothers, a shoemaker's, a blacksmith shop, a wheelwright shop, a candy store, a stone mason's, a Union Free Church, a grocery store and a small school. The inhabitants were either farmers, merchants, jacks-of-all-trades or summer residents.

The railroad station, the last stop on the Great Neck - New York route (the Port Washington, Plandome & Manhasset depots hadn't been added to the line at that time), was two miles out of town at its present site. Sam Hayden's store at the corner of Hicks Lane and Middle Neck Road was the village center.

There were no meat markets in Great Neck at the time. Meat had either to be imported from New York City or purchased from traveling meat salesman operating out of Manhasset.

During the winter there was very little commuting between New York and Great Neck. The summer residents moved back to their city homes and the Great Neck farmers had little reason to travel to the "big city"   .

But with the advent of spring a flow of horse-drawn carriages would wind their way over muddy, dirt roads to Great Neck with the belongings of the summer residents. The steamship line, dormant throughout the winter, suddenly sprang to life, chugging out its daily passage to and from New York, and the Long Island Railroad, always "reliable", and "dependent" even in the days of our forefathers, began to take on more than just a handful of passengers for the 50 minute trip to New York. Great Neck became alive in the Spring.

Great Neck was recognized, even then, as one of the most popular and swank summer resorts around New York City. A very active and formal social life thrived here. Entertainment of all sorts, teas, luncheons, card-parties, dinners, and cocktail parties occupied the residents throughout the day.

The highlight of the day was the arrival or departure of the "Sewanhaka" or the "Idlewild" sidewheelers steamboats which transported the commuting members of the town to and from New York. The "Sewanhaka" which had been running throughout the seventies (1870's), came to a sudden and unfortunate end in the eighties (1880's) when it caught fire off Hell Gate Island killing the heads of thirteen Great Neck families. Several lives were saved, however, including those of Mr. J.P. Grace and family. Mr. Grace threw his family overboard during the fire and then leaped to safety himself. Mrs. Grace was rescued despite the fact that in a heroic act, she gave her life jacket to an elderly gentleman.

After the demolition of the "Sewanhaka" the "Idlewild" was substituted. A large paddlewheel boat, similar to those used in the Hudson River tours today. It began its daily cruise at Sea Cliff, stopping at Glen Cove and Sands Point and finally Great Neck at about 8 in the morning. Once the Great Neck commuters had boarded, the boat set out for New York, skirting the coast of Long Island and then crossing the East River.

The boat schedule was not nearly as dependable as the railroad's. If the weather was inclement, the trip would often take a great deal longer than one hour, and if the Sound was engulfed in a heavy fog, the boat would often not even attempt the cruise - much to the consternation of the many school children who commuted between Great Neck and several New York private schools.

The Vessel was a large one, great enough to accommodate its store of cargo, which often consisted of horses and carriages, and passengers. Some of the more exclusive commuters had private staterooms aboard. However, the fare, which was about 50 cents, was not so steep as to discourage farmers and tradespeople from using the boat. The passengers, usually the same crowd of people, were friendly and sociable on shipboard. It was considered gauche for families to bring there lunches or breakfasts on board, but there was a snack bar for those who desired food. The trip itself was a pleasant one, especially on a clear day.

Although the Long Island Railroad was in operation simultaneously with the boat, there were several reasons why the sea trip was more popular. First of all, the train trip was a complicated procedure. A commuter had to get off the train at the East River in Long Island City and take the 34th Street ferry across the river. In those days there were no tunnels. Although the railroad was quicker and slightly cheaper than the boat, the boat cruise was much more pleasant.

Secondly, a large portion of the Great Neck population lived out toward Kings Point, on the northern section of the peninsula. In order to reach the station it was necessary for these folk to hitch up a horse and buggy and travel close to five miles to the station, a rather burdensome task for a businessman to perform each morning. The boat, leaving from nearby Steamboat Landing, was much more accessible to the Kings Point dwellers.

Steamboat Landing itself is now a part of the Merchant Marine Academy. The old boat dock is currently the main dock at the Academy. Just before the boat docked each evening, the women would compete for positions along the pier, arriving early in the afternoon to get the choicest spots. An outdoor social hour always ensued, since the women always came in person, bedecked in colorful clothes and often accompanied by grooms and footmen.

This was Great Neck in 1876. Recognize it?

Map from the book of Great Neck

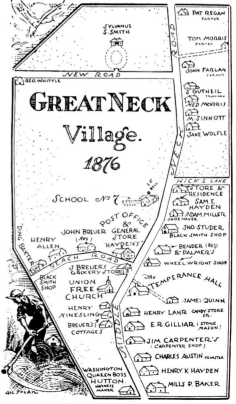

BIG PEOPLE - BIG CHANGES

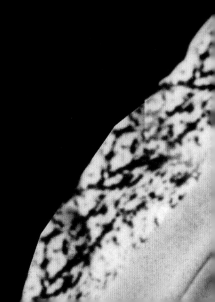

Big People - Big Changes

Roswell and Louise Eldridge and William Russell and Lilus Grace changed the face of Great Neck forever.

The Eldridges and the Graces are at least partly responsible for two incorporated villages, Great Neck's Jewish community, a bank, the library, the parks system, the Saddle Rock Grist Mill, and a vibrant Great Neck Plaza.

Roswell and Louise Eldridge resided in Redcote, a unique estate inherited by Mrs. Eldridge, who was both a Udall and a Skidmore. The Skidmores had taken control of the Redcote area around 1835, and the Udalls had taken over some property a little later. Both families were very wealthy. Redcote occupied 400 acres.

Later, Redcote became one of the first two villages to incorporate. Renamed "Saddle Rock" (after a "saddle" shaped rock directly offshore in Little Neck Bay), the mini-village consisted of the Eldridges and their servants.

Louise and Roswell were the only mayors of Saddle Rock for over 30 years, starting with its 1911 incorporation. Louise was the first female mayor in New York State. Their servants were appointed village officials.

Louise Udall Skidmore
and The Great Neck Library

In 1880, Louise Udall Skidmore, not yet married, put together a slide lecture on classical mythology, held in the home of Harriet S. Onderdonk. Admission from that, plus other fundraisers, resulted in the formation of the Great Neck Library. Working with $1000 in the treasury, Louise teamed with Mrs. Onderdonk and others, opened the library in the telegraph office,

Louise Udall Eldridge - Founding member, benefactor, president of the Great Neck Library

and appointed the telegraph operator's mother librarian.

Nine years later, the library, barely 100 books and 40 members large, incorporated as a public association library within Queens County.

The Library changed homes twice before Roswell and Louise Eldridge built and donated what is now known as the Great Neck House on Arrandale Avenue. By the end of 1907, the library's first year in its new home, its collection of books and members had grown to 2,500 and 252, respectively. Its circulation was 5,000. By the end of the 1908 circulation had reached 10,000.

Books were strictly censored. All purchases required the approval of the entire Library Board before they were bought and shelved.

In 1927, Louise Eldridge stopped her annual $1,000 donation, citing the negative impact of reliance on large gifts. The library instituted a new system, incorporating the library budget into the school budget. This system has remained in place since. Residents of the school district vote on the budget every year.

Library membership continued to grow, and with the growth came changes. The Eldridges donated two wings to the Great Neck House building in 1926, and a new children's room, reference room, and two floors of stacks in 1930. The Station, Lakeville, and Parkville branches opened in 1923, 1934, and 1954, respectively. With the final extension, the mobile library that had been in use for a long time was retired.

By 1964, membership circulation had reached 22,000 and the public demanded better facilities. A two and one-half acre plot on the corner of Bayview Avenue and Grist Mill Lane overlooking Udall's Pond was chosen. The Great Neck League of Women Voters and others requested the formation of a Library Advisory Committee, which was responsible for pro-

Devotion to the written word - Harriet Onderdonk - Founding member and first president of the Great Neck Library - 1880-1904

To meet the need, the Eldridges built and donated the Arrandale Avenue Library - Now The Great Neck House.

viding accessibility to the new library. The 45,000-square foot main branch building opened in 1970.

Free bus service to the Library was provided under the direction of the Advisory Committee. Art shows and film screenings became regular occurrences.

In 1974, music and multi-purpose rooms were created and a snack bar was added in 1978 on the lower level. A photo gallery was established in memory of Morton A. Shapiro, first chairman of the Volunteer Art Committee, in 1980.

With the formation of Levels, library Director Joseph Covino expanded the library's place in Great Neckers' lives. Formed in 1975, Levels provides a theatrical space and a wide range of after-school opportunities for local teenagers. In 1983, the Congressional Committee on Adolescence heard Levels members testify on the positive effects of Levels on their lives. Junior Levels, an extension of the program for fifth and sixth graders, was started in 1986.

Roswell Eldridge Estate

As the needs of the community continue to grow, all three library branches have recently undergone renovations.

While plans to renovate the main library as a state-of-art media center are still in the discussion stages, it is already much more than a repository of books. Its 365,323 items include books, more than 12,000 audio recordings and 9,000 videos. The library subscribes to more than 1,200 periodicals and more than 50 newspapers. There are silent study rooms, banks of computers and Internet access. Circulation has grown from 2,500 in 1907 to 710,616 and cardholders from 40 in 1889 to 32,914 in 2002. And it is a community center, replete with art exhibits, readings, movies and musical events.

The women of the Great Neck Library set out to create a large, influential library, and accomplished their mission. The library has grown exponentially over time, and has indeed become an integral part of the town.

The Graces

President) and landlord and developer of much of the property surrounding the train station.

Local lore claims that Grace acquired the land in a lawsuit from the Long Island Railroad. The story goes that one day Grace took the train (which he hardly ever did) and the bathroom door was locked. Grace sued the railroad and settled out of court for the land surrounding the railroad.

Regardless of the validity of the story, we do know that Grace owned the land, which he named Thomaston in honor of Lilus' hometown, Thomaston, Maine. Later, the area surrounding the train station was renamed Great Neck Plaza, but Thomaston still exists today, a primarily residential village with a small commercial area on the boundaries of Northern Boulevard and East Shore Road and apartment houses along South Middle Neck Road. The Grace family retained possession of most of the property for a long time, finally giving up its last share of the valuable land in 1981.

One of W.R. Grace's most longlasting contributions to Great Neck, beyond his

William Russell Grace, Irish immigrant, business heavyweight, and two-time Mayor of New York City, lived in Great Neck with his wife Lilus for a significant portion of their lives

The Graces lived on 200 acres of the old Adam Mott farm east of Blue Sea Lane in Kings Point. He called his estate Gracefield, and enjoyed the pleasures of a gorgeous Italian-tiled pool, a racetrack with a stable for the horses, and a walled garden. Grace served as Mayor of Great Neck, President of Great Neck's first bank (Roswell Eldridge was the Vice

Post-war Image of W.R. Grace

tenure as Mayor, President of the Bank of Great Neck, and realtor, was his role in bringing Jews to Great Neck. Grace brought his tailor and clothier, Abram Wolf, to Great Neck from New York City, offering him a free home.

The Merritt Post family initially gave Wolf the house free of charge, but soon they began charging rent. Wolf put up with it; it was a well situated 12-room house on 11 acres.

The family then offered to sell the house to Wolf for $11,000. When he declined, they sold it for $75,000 to someone else. It appeared his son I.G. Wolf learned from this event, and soon went into real estate. I.G. Wolf played a large role in the real estate boom of the early 20th century. The Wolf's family's presence attracted more Jewish families over the years. Today, the Jewish population of Great Neck is predominant.

Another branch of the Grace family, Mr. and Mrs. Morgan Grace, was

famous educator, to help her create a top-flight prep school. Today, the Buckley school still operates in North Hills.

Originally changes in Great Neck were due to the actions of individuals. Big

Haberdashery shop of Abram Wolf , Middle Neck Road, Old Village of Great Neck. Ca. 1891. Abram and his wife Rose and children were the first Jews to move to Great Neck. Photo courtesy of Linda Emanuel.

responsible for the creation of the Buckley school. Originally situated in Great Neck, the school was once dubbed the Great Neck Preparatory School. It was built under the leadership of Mrs. Grace, who wanted a good school for wealthy Great Neck children. Until then, some well-to-do families would move back to the city in the fall so that the children could attend a fine private school. She brought in Lord Buckley, a

names were common on the peninsula, and their initiative carried Great Neck forward. This was not the way Great Neck would operate forever. In the next century, the residents banded together, creating a vast array of organizations. Control of a town that was once held by a few significant, civic-minded individuals was seized by the masses. In the 20th century, Great Neck belonged to the people.

Mrs. Barstow's Vision

For both aesthetic and safety reasons, the grade crossing at the Great Neck Station was eliminated by 1935, under the leadership of Mrs. Florence Barstow, a leader of the Woman's Club of GreatNeck and a patron of the town's Girl Scouts. Building an overpass cost over half a million dollars, and $32,500 was donated by Mr. and Mrs. William Slocum Barstow. Seventh Street near the station was graciously re-named after them. The LIRR had wanted to elevate the tracks. It took Ira Mcknight and a group of concerned Great Neckers over ten years to convince them otherwise. Walter P. Chrysler, I.G. Wolf, Walter Davis, Frederick Gilsey and Richard Kehoe also contributed.

Florence D. Barstow
1876-1958

Though Mrs. Barstow could hardly have foreseen the swell of traffic near the station, to this day the overpass helps ease Middle Neck Road's congestion.

The train ran year-round, with almost flawless service. By 1880, Great Neck's population reached 1000, and by 1900, 2000. Businessmen began to stay for the winter, choosing a sweet, white blanket of snow over the soiled-looking drifts on the streets of Manhattan. Thus came the emergence of a suburban community.

While stagecoach service to New York began earlier than both the ferry and the train, it gained little popularity. Roads were slow, muddy, and pungent. Only with the construction of Northern Boulevard (then North Hempstead and Flushing Turnpike), which was soon serviced by trolley cars, did commuting via road pick up.

Trolley cars remained popular through the end of the First World War, when the government legalized civilian automobile purchases at a previously unseen rate. Along with these automobiles came buses, which rapidly replaced trolleys hampered by local governments' price-freezing constraints. With fares for riding trolleys frozen, profit margins began to slip, and by 1930 evidence that the trolley cars had ever existed was mostly gone. The towns and private bus companies covered the trolley tracks and took down the electric poles, replacing them with cold, hard asphalt.

The grade crossing at Middle Neck Road before 1935

The overpass helped ease congestion.

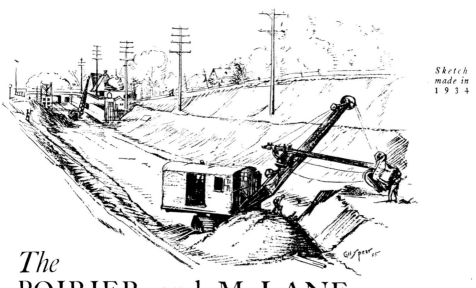

Sketch made in 1934

The
POIRIER and McLANE
CORPORATION
33 WEST 42ND STREET   **NEW YORK, N. Y.**

Point with Pride to the Grade Crossing Elimination and Lowering of the Tracks of the Railroad Station at Great Neck.

Middle Neck Road Bridge and Underpass today.

Vigilant Fire Company - North Station Plaza ca. 1910

The Turn of the Century: Great Neck Booms

Great Neck was growing at its fastest pace yet as the 20th century approached. New stores and taverns began appearing. Middle Neck Road was paved. As of 1880, there were 1,000 residents of Great Neck. By 1900, that number had doubled.

An open-air movie theater - the Airdome - opened near the Village Green in 1910. The floor was made of dirt.

The Universal Auto Bus Service offered a trip from Kings Point to the train station for only five cents and ran a special route on Sunday to accommodate Mass-goers from St. Aloysius. Horse-drawn carriages were the more expensive alternative. Great Neck was on the move.

The Airdome - Located on Middle Neck Road in the Old Village. It was used as an open-air movie theater. Patrons had to wait until it got dark. The floor was natural earth.

Middle Neck Road at Hicks Lane - 1906

Middle Neck Road looking north from the railroad station, ca. 1905

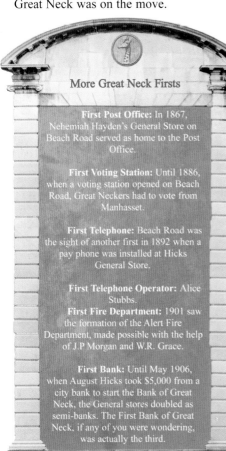

More Great Neck Firsts

First Post Office: In 1867, Nehemiah Hayden's General Store on Beach Road served as home to the Post Office.

First Voting Station: Until 1886, when a voting station opened on Beach Road, Great Neckers had to vote from Manhasset.

First Telephone: Beach Road was the sight of another first in 1892 when a pay phone was installed at Hicks General Store.

First Telephone Operator: Alice Stubbs.

First Fire Department: 1901 saw the formation of the Alert Fire Department, made possible with the help of J.P Morgan and W.R. Grace.

First Bank: Until May 1906, when August Hicks took $5,000 from a city bank to start the Bank of Great Neck, the General stores doubled as semi-banks. The First Bank of Great Neck, if any of you were wondering, was actually the third.

The Thomaston school was built on farm land in 1905 in the area now called Kensington.

In the spirit of the times, Judge Egbert LeCluse and Richard Kehoe (who had been brought in by W.R. Grace to manage his station property) pushed for improvements in public services. Paved roads, streetlights, and telephone service for Great Neck were among their concerns. In fact, the judge's general store was home to the second phone number in Great Neck. Its number? Great Neck two.

Judge LeCluse served as president of the Great Neck Improvement Society, and was known for his progressive, Rooseveltesque attitude. LeCluse, who did not hold a law degree, served as an influential judge for years.

LeCluse was 24 when he moved to Great Neck from Sayville in 1895 and became the proprietor of a general store. There were three grocery stores then, George W. Hayden, Hicks Bros. and LeCluse Bros.

"There was no such thing as bad accounts, it was a pleasure to do business in those days," Judge LeCluse said with a chuckle in an interview in the Great Neck News in 1927. "When we'd hear that a new family was coming to Great Neck, Austin Hicks and I used to mount our bicycles and tear down to the Station to meet the lady of the house or the housekeeper in charge. And how nice we'd talk to her and vie with one another for her business." He also recalled how ex-Senator John A. King, W.R. Grace and Vincent and William Brokaw would have race meets, driving their prancing steeds down Middle Neck Road.

The Fire Departments

LeCluse also teamed up with other notables to form the Alert Engine Hook and Ladder and Hose Company Number One in 1901. Among its patrons were W.R. Grace, J.P. Morgan, Walter Chrysler, George Dodge, Roswell Eldridge and Willim Gould Brokaw.

Today, the Alert Fire Department has two locations. The main station is at 555 Middle Neck Road, and the second Station is at 142 Steamboat Road. The Alert Fire Department serves the villages of Great

Alert Fire Hall. The Alert Fire Company was founded in 1901. The handsome fire hall at 555 Middle Neck Road dates from the early 1900's.

Alert Fire Dept - today.

Neck, Kings Point and Saddle Rock.

The Vigilant Fire Company, in existence before the turn of the century, was often seen borrowing other people's horses to race to a fire. The volunteer organization was officially established in 1904, under the guidance of John J. Hughes, Richard Kehoe and Claude Warner. William K. Vanderbilt, Jr. (of Lake Success) was responsible for the majority of the funding, and was often seen picking up a ladder and fighting fires.

These days, the villages of Great Neck Estates, Great Neck Plaza and Kensington, along with part of Thomaston, benefit from the service of the all volunteer fire department. Vigilant Fire Company is located at

Above - Alert Fire Dept.
Below - Manhasset-
Lakeville Fire Dept. on
Prospect St.

Above - Manhasset-
Lakeville Fire Dept.
Below - Vigilant Fire
Dept.

The Vigilants in action, helping put out a blaze on Middle
Neck Road. Note dog mascot in truck.

83 Cuttermill Road and boasts about 100
firefighters. A dispatcher is on the job 24
hours a day.

The Manhasset-Lakeville Fire District
serves part of Great Neck Plaza and
Thomaston, and all of Lake Success and
Russell Gardens. It is also an all volunteer
department, and has two locations: the
first is at Prospect Street, the second at
the corner of Jason Avenue and Northern
Boulevard. A different dispatcher is on the
job 24 hours a day.

News in Great Neck

The North Hempstead Record began printing in 1907, with its main focus on Great Neck life. announcements regarding who entertained whom and when were common in the paper, as were accounts of the goings-on of the real estate market, which were numerous.

When the Great Neck News began publication in 1925, a rivalry began. The North Hempstead Record changed names, becoming the Great Neck Record in 1933 and is now part of the Anton chain of local weeklies. Both newspapers exist to this day.

Great Neck Record

YOUR COMMUNITY NEWSPAPER

An Anton Newspaper-
Founded 1907

Serving the Communities of Great Neck, Great Neck Estates, Great Neck Plaza, Kensington, Kings Point, Lake Success, Russell Gardens, Saddle Rock and Thomaston and the Unincorporated Areas

READ!

Since 1907

THE ROARING TWENTIES

Party at F. Scott Fitzgerald's home in Great Neck, ca. 1923. Princeton University Libraries.

Roaring Twenties

"There was music from my neighbor's house through the summer nights. In his blue gardens men and women came and went like moths among the whisperings and the champagne and the stars."

Nick Carraway, F. Scott Fitzgerald's The Great Gatsby

Great Neck met the Roaring Twenties with a roar of its own. The once rural town was urbanizing at its fastest pace yet. With the tracks' electrification came faster, cheaper, and more reliable trains. Adding to the once rural community's attractiveness were good schools and parks. Even more people flocked to the peninsula.

A special 11:18 train ran for men and women of the theater, bringing them home late at night.

Broadway shows previewed at Irving M. Lesser's Playhouse Theatre on Middle Neck Road, and movies were shown down the street at the Robertson brothers' Mayfair Theater on South Station Plaza. Parties were opulent, attracting people from all over the area. Great Neck, the one-time quiet, rural town, had become a social hub.

In 1928, no suburb in America could match the Playhouse's lineup that August and September. Nor, outside of Hollywood, could any community claim such a star-studded line up of residents. Great Neck was home to numerous celebrities, and the figurative telephone book of the era included names like **Gene Buck, Fanny Brice, Eddie Cantor, Maurice Chevalier, Charlie Chaplin, Jane Cowl, Frank Craven, Will Durant, Florence Eldridge, Paulette Goddard, Oscar Hammerstein II, Sam Harris, Willie Howard, Dennis King, Groucho Marx, Marilyn Miller, Oscar Shaw, Ernest Truex and Sam Warner.**

Basil Rathbone, best known for his portrayal of Sherlock Holmes in the 1930s and 1940s, but gave outstanding performances in many, other films as

Irving M. Lesser's Great Neck Playhouse - 1920's

Charlie Chaplain - The champion of the silver screen was a familiar face in Great Neck. During the early 1900's, he made more people laugh than any other man who ever lived and changed the way people looked at the world.

Eddie Cantor - Famous radio, stage and screen star, lived on Lakeville Road. He was also proud of originating the slogan and idea for the "March of Dimes"

well. Rathbone also appeared in many plays, and his voice could be heard in numerous radio broadcasts and recordings.

George M. Cohan, the songwriter, playwright and producer, wrote *"Yankee Doodle Dandy"* while living in a mansion on Kings Point Road. After reading in the newspaper that war had been declared, Mr. Cohan wrote the melody and words to "Over There." It became the unofficial anthem of World War I.

Besides "Over There," George M. Cohan, also wrote, "You're a Grand Old Flag" and "I'm a Yankee Doodle Dandy." while living in a grand old estate in Kings Point.

1922 ad from Great Neck's golden past.

Basil Rathbone - best known for his portrayal of Sherlock Holmes. He used to have his pooch taxied around in Great Neck.

Madam, there's no such thing as a tough child - if you parboil them first for seven hours, they always come out tender.
W.C. Fields

W.C. Fields on location filming "Sally of the Sawdust" in 1925. Quoted "Once ... in the wilds of Afghanistan, I lost my corkscrew, and we were forced to live on nothing but food and water for days."

Here's to our wives and girl-friends...may they never meet!
Groucho Marx

Years later, Cohan said in an interview: "Funny about them giving me a medal. All I wrote was a bugle call." "Over There" swept America and the world. A month after publication, it was being hummed, sung, and whistled in every corner of the United States.

Another of Cohan's well-loved tunes, "45 Minutes from Broadway," was the story of his daily commute to Manhattan from Great Neck. He lived in Great Neck from 1914 to 1925.

W.C. Fields, one of America's greatest comedians, moved to Melborne Road in Russell Gardens in

Maurice Chevalier-was the quintessential Frenchman. He introduced the world to such memorable songs as "Louise," "Mimi," and, from the Academy Award-winning film, Gigi, "Thank Heaven for Little Girls."

Oscar Hammerstein II - Librettist, lyricist & producer, lived in Kennilworth in a house now owned by Alan King.

September, 1928. He was one of America's greatest comedians; a master mimic whose humor and acerbic wit was accompanied by a unique combination of a snarling drawl, wooden expression, and flawlessly timed gestures. He knew how to make audiences laugh. His careers in burlesque, vaudeville, the stage, on the silent screen and in talking motion pictures and radio were among the command performances of the twentieth century.

Born William Claude Dukenfield, the eldest of five children in a poor family, W.C. Fields quit school after four years to help his father sell vegetables from a horse cart. He left home at age 11, living on the streets and making do with stolen food and clothing. He spent many nights in jail. By age 13, W.C. Fields was a pool shark and skilled juggler. He landed his first gig as an entertainer at an amusement park in Pennsylvania.

"If at first you don't succeed, try, try, and try again. Then give up. There's no use being a damned fool about it," Fields was known to say.

To attract crowds while working as a juggler in Atlantic City, W.C. Fields pretended to be drowning. He didn't need such gimmicks for long. At age 23, the great pantomimist and comedian played with Sarah Bernhardt and Houdini. He starred at the Folies-Bergere, with a youthful Charlie Chaplin and Maurice Chevalier on the program.

From 1915 through 1921, he was in each of the Ziegfeld Follies. In 1935, he captured the essence of the fastidious Dickens' character Mr. Micawber in

Walter Percy Chrysler - 1875-1940, Auto magnate who worked his way up though the ranks. He lived in Great Neck beginning in 1923 on a magnificent estate, which he bequeathed to the USMMA.

Ed Wynn - 1886-1966, was America's "perfect fool." He loved his homes in Great Neck. He both acted in and wrote material for the Ziegfeld Follies.

Eddie Cantor's Estate
Great Neck, L. I., *to be sold at*

Auction

Sat., June 3, at 3 p. m. on premises

Ten acres . . . beautifully developed and land-scaped; a 2½-story fire-proof and sound-proof English Tudor Mansion, built in 1929; 17 main rooms, finished basement, concealed radiators, vapor (oil-burning) heat; 2-story garage with 2 apartments above. Located about one mile south of the Great Neck Railroad Station, directly opposite the Lakeville Golf Club.

Offered in 2 parcels, one consisting of the mansion and garage, the other, the remaining acreage for building site on Middle Neck Road, and as a whole.

75% on mortgage . . . 5 years.

Joseph P. Day Inc.
Auctioneer
67 Liberty Street, New York City
Telephone - BArclay 7-7000

W.C. Fields - The funniest thing about comedy is that you never know why people laugh. I know what makes them laugh, but trying to get your hands on the why of it is like trying to pick an eel out of a tub of water."
-- W. C. Fields

MGM's *David Copperfield. The Bank Dick* came out in 1940. The next year he starred in *Never Give a Sucker an Even Break*. W. C. Fields deadpan humor also worked on the radio, as the nemesis of Edgar Bergen's wooden dummy Charlie McCarthy.

W.C. Fields made 50 films. His first, a 15-minute flick called *Pool Sharks*, was made when he was 36. He wrote, acted and directed the classic 1940 comedy *My Little Chickadee*, in which he appeared with Mae West.

"Start every day with a smile, and get it over with," W. C. Fields said.

He had bite and edge. It made W. C. Fields a star. W. C. Fields died in California on Dec. 25, 1946.

The moniker **Joan Crawford** came from a film studio publicity contest but the actress with the mocking eyes quickly made her mark.

She had worked as a laundress, waitress and shopgirl before she won a Charleston contest and joined the chorus line of a Broadway show, this girl from San Antonio named Lucille Le Sueur. An MGM scout noticed her and signed her to a film contract. The epitome of glamour and one of Hollywood' celluloid queens, Joan Crawford starred in more than 80 films during her 50-year career. Hard-edged and strong-willed, she was known for sometimes scrubbing her own floors.

Crawford's first role as a starlet was in *Our Dancing Daughters* in 1928. She was a sensual, flamboyant flapper on the silent screen, the ideal Jazz Age girl. In the 1930's, her star soared. She played romantic leads opposite Gary Cooper, Spencer Tracy and Clark Gable in films like the 1931 *Dance, Fools, Dance* and *The Women* in 1939.

D.W. Griffith and W.C. Fields filming Sally of the Sawdust. Darley and Dunster Road near Middle Neck Road. (Russell Gardens) ca. 1925

Joan Crawford's main residence was Hollywood but Crawford lived for a time in a mansion on Station Road in Great Neck.

After a brief dip in popularity, in 1945 she won an Academy Award for best actress in *Mildred Pierce*. The role was quintessential Crawford: a strong, mature and incredibly glamorous woman struggling with love and career. Later she played the anguished older woman. Crawford became a legend.

Criticized in *Mommy Dearest* for being quite strict with her four adopted children, she married and divorced three actors -- Douglas Fairbanks Jr., Franchot Tone and Philip Terry. Her final marriage was to Alfred Steele, president of Pepsi-Cola. Crawford died in 1977.

Charlie Chaplin was one of the most famous stars in motion picture history. Born in 1889 into a poor London family, Chaplin was told at a young age that he had talent. He soon began to believe it with a passion. By age 10 he was working as a mime.

Chaplin came to the United States in 1910 to tour as a variety and music hall performer. Undoubtedly best known for his portrayal of *The Tramp*, released in 1914, Chaplin's signature mustache, derby hat, baggy pants, penguin waddle and slapstick antics would thereafter always be recognizable. The funniest man in the world hit the A-list. Films such as *The Kid* (1920), in which he reprised the Tramp, became legendary. Chaplin's Tramp grew in depth and complexity over the years to become a powerful icon and symbol of man against the world.

While living in Great Neck, Chaplin courted the actress Paulette Goddard. She became his third wife. Along with the actors Douglas Fairbanks, Sr., and Mary Pickford and the director D. W. Griffith, Chaplin formed the United Artists film corporation in 1919. By the following year, Chaplin was earning $10,000 per week, an astronomical amount in those days.

Chaplin wrote and directed nearly all his films. The Tramp also reappeared in classic films such as

Charlie Chaplain standing on a train platform, ca. 1925. Photo courtesy Chicago Historical Society.

The Gold Rush (1925) as well as his first two sound films, *City Lights* and *Modern Times*. Released in 1936, the film also made Paulette Goddard a star.

Chaplin played two roles in the 1940 satire T*he Great Dictator*, a Jewish barber who fought in World War I and the evil Adenoid Hynkel, a dictator basis on Adolf Hitler. He played a sardonic mass murderer in the 1947 film *Monsieur Verdoux*. Because of his thinly veiled political views, rumors of Chaplin being a Communist sympathizer swirled, causing Chaplin to settle in Switzerland. The king of silent comedy returned to the United States to receive an Oscar in 1972.

Even amid the accusations, his troubled loves and marriages, Charlie Chaplin made a profound impact on everyone's life in the early 1900's. He made more people laugh than any other man who had ever lived. His films provoked sympathy and understanding for the underdog, while at the same time reflecting sophistication and style. In one of his most indelible moments in *The Gold Rush*, Chaplin and a friend are so hungry that they boil a pair of shoes. Chaplin polishes his plate with his sleeve, ladles snow on his shoes like a delicate sauce, swirls the shoelaces on his fork like pasta and eats the shoes as if they were fine caviar.

Chaplin makes it seem as if were one of the most delicious meals that he ever enjoyed .

In retrospect, the master comedian was really making films about himself.

Charlie Chaplin was knighted in 1975. He died of natural causes two years later at his home in Switzerland on Christmas Day. He was 88 years old.

CHARLES CHAPLIN

Faces of Great Neck:
F. Scott Fitzgerald

F. Scott Fitzgerald's house in Great Neck Estates as it appeared in 1922.

The writer F. Scott Fitzgerald placed Gatsby, his famous work's doomed dreamer, at the tip of Kings Point in his tale of the corruption of the American dream.

But contrary to local lore, Francis Scott Key Fitzgerald did not pen The Great Gatsby while living in Great Neck. Fitzgerald actually wrote his book while in Valescure, on the French Riviera. The author based West Egg, the novel's main setting, on Great Neck, and modeled East Egg on Sands Point.

In 1922, before moving to France, Fitzgerald, his wife Zelda, and daughter, rented space at Gateway Drive in Great Neck Estates. They chose Great Neck for the same reason many of the celebrities of the twenties chose it: Great Neck was close to the theater, yet in the country.

The Fitzgeralds immersed themselves in Great Neck's social scene, which was at its peak during their residency. He gained the

F. Scott Fitzgerald and his wife Zelda from a Broadway production of "The Great Gatsby," by Owen Davis, 1926

friendship of Ring Lardner, a sports-writer and humorist.

Fitzgerald's play, *The Vegetable,* failed within a year. F. Scott, already an established writer, with *The Beautiful and the Damned,* as well as shorter pieces for The Saturday Evening Post under his belt, composed short stories for significant sums for magazines.

F. Scott and Zelda soon drank themselves out of a considerable amount of money. Domestic bouts often ended with Zelda staying the night at the Lardners'. In order to get away from the distractions of Great Neck and New York, the family moved to Valescure in the spring of 1924.

On April 23, 1930, Zelda, fearful that her taxi would not make it to ballet lessons on time, exited the car and ran through the streets of Paris in her ballet clothes. Her husband checked her into a mental hospital, only to have Zelda check herself out in May.

The Fitzgeralds never returned to live in Great Neck, though they did come back to the United States, settling in Hollywood, Montgomery, and Delaware, among other places. Early in 1932, Zelda suffered a mental relapse, and spent the rest of her life checking in and out of mental health hospitals.

Fitzgerald underwent the worst period of his life, and drank as he never had before. He floated from place to place, trying his hand at Hollywood occasionally. He was ill, poor, and depressed. F. Scott Fitzgerald, literary giant — and one-time Great Neck resident — died of a heart attack in Hollywood on December 21, 1940.

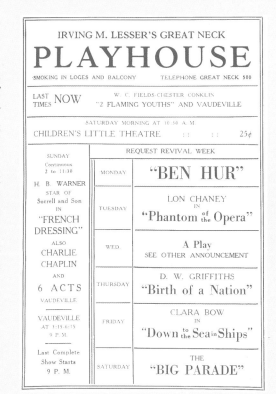

Irving M. Lesser's Great Neck Playhouse - 1920's

Avalon sign painted by Gotfred Nilsson, advertising a new housing development in Thomaston. Great Neck was on the move.

ZELDA FITZGERALD AND THE JAZZ AGE

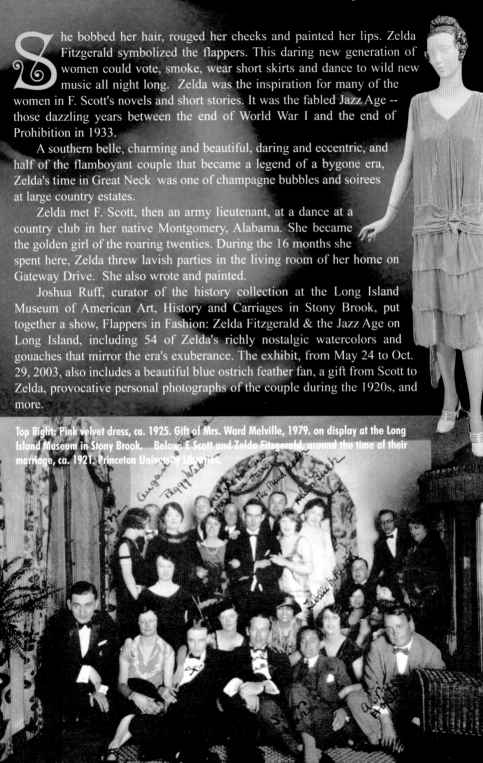

She bobbed her hair, rouged her cheeks and painted her lips. Zelda Fitzgerald symbolized the flappers. This daring new generation of women could vote, smoke, wear short skirts and dance to wild new music all night long. Zelda was the inspiration for many of the women in F. Scott's novels and short stories. It was the fabled Jazz Age -- those dazzling years between the end of World War I and the end of Prohibition in 1933.

A southern belle, charming and beautiful, daring and eccentric, and half of the flamboyant couple that became a legend of a bygone era, Zelda's time in Great Neck was one of champagne bubbles and soirees at large country estates.

Zelda met F. Scott, then an army lieutenant, at a dance at a country club in her native Montgomery, Alabama. She became the golden girl of the roaring twenties. During the 16 months she spent here, Zelda threw lavish parties in the living room of her home on Gateway Drive. She also wrote and painted.

Joshua Ruff, curator of the history collection at the Long Island Museum of American Art, History and Carriages in Stony Brook, put together a show, Flappers in Fashion: Zelda Fitzgerald & the Jazz Age on Long Island, including 54 of Zelda's richly nostalgic watercolors and gouaches that mirror the era's exuberance. The exhibit, from May 24 to Oct. 29, 2003, also includes a beautiful blue ostrich feather fan, a gift from Scott to Zelda, provocative personal photographs of the couple during the 1920s, and more.

Top Right: Pink velvet dress, ca. 1925. Gift of Mrs. Ward Melville, 1979. on display at the Long Island Museum in Stony Brook.   Below: F. Scott and Zelda Fitzgerald, around the time of their marriage, ca. 1921. Princeton University Libraries.

The wife of F. Scott Fitzgerald, who put her in two brilliant novels, "This Side of Paradise" and "The Beautiful and Damned," does not need to join the Lucy Stone League in order to identify herself as a personality. Everything Zelda Fitzgerald says and does stands out

PHOTOGRAPH BY GORDON BRYANT

Eulogy on the Flapper

By Zelda Sayre Fitzgerald

pleasant and what they please, but simply to outdo the founders of the Honorable Order of Flappers; to outdo *everything*. Flapperdom has become a game; it is no longer a philosophy.

I came across an amazing editorial a short time ago. It fixed the blame for all divorces, crime waves, high prices, unjust taxes, violations of the Volstead Act and crimes in Hollywood upon the head of the Flapper. The paper wanted back the dear old fireside of long ago, wanted to resuscitate "Hearts and Flowers" and have it instituted as the sole tune played at dances from now on and forever, wanted prayers before breakfast on Sunday morning—and to bring things back to this superb state it advocated restraining the Flapper. All neurotic "women of thirty" and all divorce cases, according to the paper, could be traced to the Flapper. As a matter of fact, she hasn't yet been given a chance. I know of no divorcées or neurotic women of thirty who were ever Flappers. Do you? And I should think that fully airing the desire for unadulterated gaiety, for romances that she knows will not last, and for dramatizing herself would make her more inclined to favor the "back to the fireside" movement than if she were repressed until age gives her those rights that only youth has the right to give.

I refer to the right to experiment with herself as a transient, poignant figure who will be dead tomorrow. Women, despite the fact that nine out of ten of them go through life with a death-bed air either of snatching-the-last-moment or with martyr-resignation, do not die tomorrow—or the next day. They have to live on to any one of many bitter ends, and I should think the sooner they learned that things weren't going to be over until they were too tired to care, the quicker the divorce court's popularity would decline.

"Out with inhibitions," gleefully shouts the Flapper, and elopes with the Arrow-collar boy that she had been thinking, for a week or two, might make a charming breakfast companion. The marriage is annulled by the proverbial irate parent and the Flapper comes home, none the worse for wear, to marry, years later, and live happily ever afterwards.

I see no logical reasons for keeping the young illusioned. Certainly disillusionment comes easier at twenty than at forty—the fundamental and inevitable disillusionments, I mean. Its effects on the Flappers I have known have simply been to crystallize their ambitious desires and give form to their code of living so that they *can* come home and live happily ever afterwards—or go into the movies or become social service "workers" or something. Older people, except a few geniuses, artistic and financial, simply throw up their hands, heave a great many heart-rending sighs and moan to themselves something about what a hard thing life is—and then, of course, turn to their children and wonder why they don't believe in Santa Claus and the kindness of their fellow men and in the tale that they will be happy if they are good and obedient. And yet the strongest cry against Flapperdom is that it is making the youth of the country cynical. It is making them intelligent and teaching them to capitalize their natural resources and get their money's worth. They are merely applying business methods to being young.

THE Flapper is deceased. Her outer accoutrements have been bequeathed to several hundred girls' schools throughout the country, to several thousand big-town shop-girls, always imitative of the several hundred girls' schools, and to several million small-town belles always imitative of the big-town shop-girls via the "novelty stores" of their respective small towns. It is a great bereavement to me, thinking as I do that there will never be another product of circumstance to take the place of the dear departed.

I am assuming that the Flapper will live by her accomplishments and not by her Flapping. How can a girl say again, "I do not want to be respectable because respectable girls are not attractive," and how can she again so wisely arrive at the knowledge that "boys *do* dance most with the girls they kiss most," and that "men *will* marry the girls they could kiss before they had asked papa?" Perceiving these things, the Flapper awoke from her lethargy of sub-deb-ism, bobbed her hair, put on her choicest pair of earrings and a great deal of audacity and rouge and went into the battle. She flirted because it was fun to flirt and wore a one-piece bathing suit because she had a good figure, she covered her face with powder and paint because she didn't need it and she refused to be bored chiefly because she wasn't boring. She was conscious that the things she did were the things she had always wanted to do. Mothers disapproved of their sons taking the Flapper to dances, to teas, to swim and most of all to heart. She had mostly masculine friends, but youth does not need friends—it needs only crowds, and the more masculine the crowds the more crowded for the Flapper. Of these things the Flapper was well aware!

Now audacity and earrings and one-piece bathing suits have become fashionable and the first Flappers are so secure in their positions that their attitude toward themselves is scarcely distinguishable from that of their débutante sisters of ten years ago toward *themselves*. They have won their case. They are blasé. And the new Flappers galumping along in unfastened galoshes are striving not to do what is

F. Scott Fitzgerald Lived Here

When the Brilliant Author of the "Great Gatsby" Resided in Great Neck, He Couldn't get Along On $36,000 a year. Here's Why.

By Martha Wiley

Recently, when a Kensington housewife entered the Great Neck Library and asked for a novel by the late F. Scott Fitzgerald, the librarian's reply was, "Sorry! All his books are out!"

As the disappointed woman started for the door, the librarian added: "You should have come in several months ago. All the Fitzgerald books were gathering dust then! But now we've had such a demand we've had to send for reprints, and there's a waiting list a mile long for them!"

There were no waiting lists for Fitzgerald's books just before his untimely death in 1940, when he passed away obscurely and forgotten. The cause of the public's revived interest in him is a couple of current best sellers – his biography, "*The far side of Paradise*," authored by Arthur Mizener, and his pseudo-biography, "*The Disenchanted*," written by Budd Schulberg, of "What Makes Sammy Run?" fame.

It was during the celebrated Jazz Age, while F. Scott Fitzgerald was still the handsome young god of American letters, that he chose the suburb of Great Neck for his home. In October, 1922, the Fitzgerald family rented a $300-a-month tan stucco house on Gateway drive, in the Estates.

The house was occupied by Scott, his beautiful wife Zelda, their one-year old Daughter Scottie, and three servants. Most of the time the house was also occupied by a continual ebb and flow of guests. It was a hectic household. The vivacious Zelda despised domestic responsibilities and, although their servants were unsatisfactory, Scott was one of those compassionate employers who are unable to criticize or fire a bad employee. The servants, too, had a hard time of it, having to live in close proximity to a pair of non-conforming geniuses who did everything and anything to excess.

Two of the Fitzgeralds' excessive habits were drinking and party-throwing. Their set of Rules for Guests which they jestingly concocted contained such items as "*Visitors are requested not to break down the doors in search of liquor, even when authorized to do so by the host and hostess,*" and "*Weekend guests are respectfully notified that invitations to stay over Monday, issued by the host and hostess during the small hours of Sunday morning, must not be taken seriously!*"

Fitzgerald's Great Neck parties were marathon events, lasting for days. often the revelry would begin in a Manhattan night club, where Scott would collect a mixed group of bootleggers, confused strangers, indignant friends, theatrical and literary notables and veteran Lost Weekenders. They would be packed into the Fitzgeralds' second-hand Rolls Royce and the perilous ride home would begin.

Scott and Zelda were reckless drivers and tore up Northern Boulevard as if possessed by demons. They would amuse their human cargo by driving on the wrong side of the Street, or steering their vehicle into a pond!

Once, when a Douglaston police officer arrested Zelda for speeding, she retorted, *"Stick 'em up, bud! I'm the Bobhaired Bandit!"*

The Gateway Drive neighbors had a fine time gossiping: *"I got up this morning and walked up the street, and there they were, curled up together on their front lawn, snoring! Who? Why, those awful Fitzgeralds, of course!"*

But personages of world-renown, recognizing Scott's crazy antics as an escape-valve for his creative drive, thronged to his home. Many a world-weary Manhattanite helped to enliven the Fitzgerald festivities. Among these were Van Wyck Brooks, Gloria Swanson, H. L. Mencken, Sherwood Anderson and Dorothy Parker. But it was Ring Lardner who became Scott's closest chum during the Great Neck days. Ring Larder joked about his pal in a review, when he wrote about how "Scott can be seen most any day on the streets of Great Neck Leashing high-bred dogs because he can't bear to see any of them untied!" The basis for this remark was Zelda's huge pet, a prize-winning police dog name Fritzi. The eternal bills and their super extravaganzas soon made Scott realize that it was impossible for them to live in Great Neck for less than $36,000 a year! But he didn't start worrying yet. There were the royalties from his two novels, and then *"This Side of Paradise"* was sold to the movies for $10,000. So their whirlwind spending continued. Gateway Drive continued to receive a stream of international celebrities, all seeing their share of pink elephants.

But finally, one fine morning, F. Scott Fitzgerald got out of bed, rubbed his head, glanced in his checkbook, and noticed he was $5,000 in debt. Immediately he went on the wagon and went to work. Over their garage was a big room, empty except for an oil stove. Here Fitzgerald hibernated during the entire winter, often working for twelve hours a stretch. By April he had produced eleven stories for the *Saturday Evening Post* and earned over $17,000! But he moaned later, "I worked hard as hell last winter, but it was all trash and it nearly broke my heart as well as my iron constitution!"

Actually some of the stories were excellent, and several appear in the new anthology of his best work. But Scott was depressed. He told Zelda that he was sick of having maids bullying them, sick of tradesmen trying to snare them. And, of course, he

One of the last pictures of F. Scott Fitzgerald was taken in 1937, three years before he died. The photographer was Carl Van Vechten, his old friend of the hectic '20s.

was sick of always being over his head financially. What he did not realize, then, was that he already had the habit. Never again was he to be free of debt.

In his late thirties, Fitzgerald felt an inertia of dried-up emotions assail him. He called it "an emotional crack-up," and wrote, "I felt like the beady-eyed men I used to see on the commuting train from Great Neck. I was one with them now, one with the smooth articles who said: *"I'm sorry, but business is business!"*

Since Great Neck was and is a suburb filled primarily with businessmen, it is probable that Fitzgerald often felt like an alien. In common with most creative artists, he felt a half-superior, half inferior emotion when in contact with the efficient executive, the hearty salesman, the professional extrovert. *"They're so stable,"* he thought. For F. Scott Fitzgerald was as unstable as could be, but he understood himself completely, and out of his introspection he wrote many a perfect line.

He loved Great Neck, though, for at that time he and Zelda were happily in love. They spent almost three ecstatic years here, watching their daughter learn to walk and talk. During his subsequent travels, F. Scott Fitzgerald was never again to know such contentment.

He set down part of his yearning for it when he made Great Neck the locale for his most acclaimed novel, *"The Great Gatsby."* Through the book descriptive passages sing his nostalgia for our lovely Long Island town, with it's fabulous landscapes and fabulous residents.

In April, 1924, when the Fitzgeralds moved from Great Neck to Paris, Ring Lardner sent a farewell poem to Zelda which ended:
"To hell with Scott Fitzgerald then!
To hell with Scott his daughter!
It's you and I back home again
To Great Neck where men are men
And booze is 3/4 water!"

F. Scott Fitzgerald never returned to the village he loved. He dined in Rome, wined on the Riviera, suffered insomnia in a succession of countries, tended his insane wife in Alabama, and died lonely in Hollywood at the age of 44, all his books long out of print.

Perhaps his ghost is wandering on the edges of our town, chuckling over it's memories, and marveling at the sunset on the Sound.

Faces of Great Neck:
Ring Lardner

R ing Lardner, born Ringgold Wilmer Lardner, was already a success upon his arrival in Great Neck in 1920.

Lardner met his wife, Ellis Abbot, in 1907. They married in January of 1911. Ring Lardner, Jr., a future writer and the third of four boys, was born in 1915.

Lardner began his journalism career the year he met Ellis, and had covered St. Louis, Boston, and Chicago by 1919. His daily sports column in the Chicago Tribune, *In the Wake of the News,* was nationally syndicated, appearing in over 115 newspapers for six years.

His hit series of short stories, *You Know Me, Al,* which appeared in The Saturday Evening Post, was published in 1916. His satirical account of a Bush Leaguer's life captivated a country, forever changing the place of baseball in the hearts of Americans.

Gullibles Travels was released in 1917, and *Treat 'Em Rough* a year later. His stories amused the general public and fascinated critics. Lardner successfully meshed sports with life to create a new style of satire. He had joined the ranks of Mark Twain and Sinclair Lewis; he was a social commentator for both the common and sophisticated man by the time he was 35.

Lardner and his family arrived at Greenwich, Connecticut from Chicago in the fall of 1919, and moved to Great Neck shortly thereafter. The move was made in order to be closer to the New York theater scene. Great Neck proved to be a perfect place to suit that purpose.

Originally from Michigan, Lardner tried his hand at dozens of plays, most never produced, while living in a mansion on East Shore Road. His involvement in Great Neck and the theater extended to the point where in 1929 he teamed up with fellow Gold Coaster George M. Cohan to compose a semi-autobiographical play, *Hurry Kane.*

The writer quickly became acquainted with what he called the "social cesspool" of Long Island, and befriended the Franklin P. Adams, the Fitzgeralds, and H.B. Swope. Great Neck also offered him the proximity of his brother Rex and childhood friend Arthur Jacks.

In 1924, Lardner, following the advice of F. Scott Fitzgerald, published *How to Write Short Stories* [With Samples]. The book was a hit.

The summer of 1926 was a trying one as Lardner discovered that he had tuberculosis. This development did not slow Lardner down, however. The often-caustic writer worked doubly hard, attempting to ensure his legacy and his family's financial security.

Due to the aggravation it had caused him for years, in 1927, Lardner dropped his weekly column. He moved to East Hampton that year.

Recurring tuberculosis, coupled with heart problems, sent Lardner to a number of hospitals throughout the last five years of his life. Ring Lardner, American icon and literary revolutionary, died at his East Hampton home on September 25, 1933. He was 48 years old.

Captain Frederick Russell

Russell Gardens Advertisment, The Great Neck News 1950's

In 1921, the Station Improvement Corporation took it upon themselves to develop the area surrounding the train station. In June of 1925, the Long Island Railroad opened a new railroad station at the cost of $50,000. The Schenck farm, purchased by **Captain Frederick Russell** in 1893, was developed, and by 1926 75% of the lots in Russell Gardens had been sold. Apartments were put up all around Great Neck Plaza, as real estate investors salivated over the potential growth of the Great Neck peninsula.

In 1925, the North Hempstead Record looked back at how times had changed:

"**William G. Genner** of Arrandale Avenue has in his possession a photograph which is special interest at this time when the opening of a new railroad station in Great Neck is rapidly approaching. Mr. Genner's picture is one taken by him some eighteen years ago, showing the station with steam trains standing at the platforms, and a number of horse-drawn "buggies" waiting for returning passengers. Quite a contrast to the picture presented at commuting time nowadays when automobiles are so thick that it almost seems a miracle that their drivers can get away without mishap."

In September of 1928, **Walter W. Davis** sold his property on South Station Plaza and Middle Neck Road to Frank H. Knighton, Ralph W. McPhee, George Nicols and William H. Ross. Building plans were immediately set, with one of the potential edifices a new post office.

A new influx of immigrants hit the town, and soon plans for a Jewish religious school in the Kensington school building were underway. Kensington elementary, or Kensington Johnson School, opened on the corner of Bond and Stoner in 1921, and serviced the entire peninsula. The school had a fantastic reputation, and educated many a celebrity's offspring. Great Neck was soon home for Italian and Polish families. A new era of diversity had begun.

Chrysler Garage ca. 1920's - 124 South Middle Neck Road.

Excerpt from the 1959 Book "Groucho and Me"
written by Groucho Marx

MEANWHILE, BACK AT THE RANCH HOUSE

For those readers who are not happy with an autobiography unless the author throws in a fistful of vital statistics from time to time, this chapter is disrespectfully submitted. Besides, my meddling editor forced me. He insists he can't bill the book as an autobiography unless I tell something about myself. Frankly, I can think of much spicier subjects.

In the latter half of the twenties then, to whom it may concern, my sex was male, my height was five-feet-eight, my hair was a grizzled black, my eyes gray, my weight 153 ½ stripped (which wasn't often enough), and I was living in a ten-room house in Great Neck, Long Island, with a wife and two small children. One son named Arthur and one daughter named Miriam, if you really insist on the details.

This son had appeared on the scene around the time that the Eighteenth Amendment became the law of the land. It's not much to be proud of, but during the thirteen years of prohibition I believe my son, Arthur, held the distinction of being the youngest bootlegger in America.

Prohibition did many things to me. Not only to me but to the rest of the nation. I'm sure that many well-meaning people who voted for it, and approved of it, did so because they were convinced that it would only be a few weeks before everybody would smash their remaining booze bottles against the wall and take the pledge.

This isn't a particularly novel observation, but the world is full of people who think they can manipulate the lives of others merely by getting a law passed. There are large groups in America who, if they could swing it, would prohibit the use of everything that they didn't personally approve of - smoking, drinking, dancing, going to the movies, eating Italian salami and, if it could be regulated, even love.

The day the big blow fell, I started to spend a good deal of my time negotiating with silk-shirted bootleggers for their watered-down booze with expensive labels. They assured me that this stuff was "right off the boat." From the way it burned my gullet on the way down, I guess it was right off the boat--just scraped off the sides and bottled.

In 1926, I was living in Great Neck, and commuting to the theatre. Talk about Sodom and Gomorrah, Fire Island or Hollywood, five years after the Volstead Act became law a good percentage of the crowd I ran with on Long Island spent most of their time getting crocked. I was still a moderate drinker, not because I was eager to obey the law, but because I was afraid that if I drank too much of the rotgut that was being peddled, I would die before my time.

I went to parties where around 2 A.M., or even earlier, the guests would be stacked up like cordwood. Oh, I know you can get just as drunk today (or even tomorrow), and if you are an earnest drinker you can wake up the next morning with a good-sized hang-over, but at least you're drinking whisky. And real whisky won't kill you unless you're a pig.

Despite the fact that the drinking of fire-water is now legal, America still seems self-conscious about it. You can't advertise it on TV, not even on the late, late shows that don't come on until after midnight. In the magazine ads, for example, no one comes right out and says, "Brother, if you want to get stinking drunk, Old Snake Bite is the booze for you." No, they warily circle around the truth like a man locked in a small room with a wounded wildcat.

With Best Wishes
Groucho Marx

Well, enough social philosophy. To get back to Great Neck, many of those who couldn't afford to pay the overblown prices the bootleggers were charging, now decided to make their own joy juice. I had a friend (now dead) who used to mix orange juice with grenadine and then, as an added fillip, drop ten or fifteen drops of Ethyl gasoline into the mixture.

One day, my father came to the house. When I offered him a drink he shook his head. "Groucho," he said, "why do you drink that rotten gin? Why don't you drink wine?"

"Look, Pop," I answered, "the wine you get nowadays is just as bad as the booze. I might just as well drink grain alcohol."

He smiled. "Listen, Groucho, you know I come

Here I am in Great Neck, Long Island. The suburban squire, with rumble seat, plus fours and the face of a saint.

from France. Not Paris or Marseilles, but from the wine country. I can make you a wine that's as good as any of the vintage wines you could get here before prohibition."

"How are you going to make wine?" I asked. "You know grapes are out of season." I don't use grapes," he answered. "You can make wine without grapes? That's a good trick, if you can do it!" "Grapes are old-fashioned," he declared. "I use white raisins and malt. You get me three dozen wine bottles and corks and I'll make you a vintage wine in three weeks that will have such a bouquet you won't be able to keep your friends away from the house." Pop's face lighted up. "Maybe we go in business together. Marx's wine, made with white raisins, malt and a secret formula. We'll have stores all over the world!"

This last statement had a familiar ring.

"Pop," I said, "you may have stores all over the world, but you won't have them in the United States."

"Nonsense!" he replied. "They can't stop you from making a little wine. It's against the law? Nonsense! Anything you make in your own home is your own private business. And if they try to interfere with us," he added, "I'll sue the government for every nickel they've got!" He looked at me craftily. "You know you can do that now under a new law that's just been passed. It's called the Mann Act."

The next morning Pop happily made his way down to the cellar, lugging along eight feet of rubber hose, assorted corks, bottles, raisins, malt and a large canvas bag.

"Pop," I asked, "what's in the bag?"

"Groucho," he answered," even though you're my own son, I can't tell you that. That's my secret." Poking the bag significantly, he added, "That's the stuff that does the trick! Everyone else who makes wine just uses raisins and malt. But without this stuff"-- he poked the bag again -- "all they get is white dishwater. You wait. Marx's Wine Importers and Exporters. We'll make millions!"

About five o'clock that afternoon the mysterious concoction was finished and all the bottles were neatly stacked, cork down, against the wall. My father looked pretty beat when he came up out of the basement. "Groucho," he asked, "do you know you have rats down there?"

"Of course," I replied. "Where do you want me to have them--in the living room?"

"Why don't you try getting rid of them?" he

went on, completely unaware that I had just unloaded a terrific joke.

"I've tried getting rid of them, but it's a hopeless job. You see, Pop, our house is right near the corner, just a few feet away from a sewer. The rats evidently come up out of the sewer and get into our cellar through some subterranean passage. I've had exterminators from all parts of Long Island. They've set traps and they've sprinkled poison around. I don't think there's anything they haven't tried, but nothing has helped."

Groucho lived in this 10 room house in Thomaston in 1926.

"You know," he said, "while I was filling the bottles a rat jumped over my knee."

"Yes, Pop, I know. He's one of the best jumpers we have down there. I've been thinking seriously of entering him in the Olympic Games next year."

Whenever I had to go downstairs to stoke the furnace, I always armed myself with a baseball bat. I once killed four rats in one day. I became pretty good at it. It was either them or me, and since I had paid for the house and the rats hadn't it seemed only fair that my interests take precedence over theirs.

One night, about three weeks later, I had just gone to bed when there was a terrific roar and the house shook as though an earthquake had struck. Quickly putting on the bottom half of my pajamas (and now you know how I sleep! . . . talk about your candid autobiographies!) I rushed downstairs and joined the rest of my family who were making a mad dash for the front door.

There was no one else in the street. "That's odd," I thought. "This must be a private earthquake. Apparently mine was the only house visited."

We stood outside, quivering with cold and fright and fearful that the quake might play a return engagement. When day broke, we nervously crept back to our beds. Around noon my father arrived.

"What's the matter?" he asked. "You all look sick. Something happen?"

"Pop," I said, "at three o'clock this morning an earthquake struck our house and we haven't had any sleep."

"An earthquake? Hmmm. What you all need is a good, stiff drink of my wine," he said. "That's why I'm here. Today the three weeks is up and the wine is ready."

He should have come a day earlier. What we thought was an earthquake was just my father's wine exploding. Broken glass and corks were strewn all over the cellar and the wine was flowing as though it was New Year's Eve on an expense account. In addition to all the debris, a dozen rats were sleeping the sleep of the dead. At first I thought they were drunk, but there wasn't a hiccup in the group, so I assumed they were connoisseurs of wine and didn't care much for my father's vintage.

I never did get to drink that wine. But during the eight years we lived in the Great Neck house, we never saw a rat again. Although I have no way of knowing, I am now inclined to believe that the secret ingredient in my father's mysterious canvas bag was the first step toward the hydrogen bomb.

Great Estates

Names like "Nirvana," "Deepdale," and "The Cove", were the homes of some of America's leading industrialists. Chrysler, Vanderbilt and Proctor, to name a few. Starting from the turn of the Nineteenth century through the 1920's, these great estates rose on the former farm lands of Great Neck, transforming it into the "Jewel of the Gold Coast." Though many of these grand estates have been lost, their cultural influence on Great Neck and Long Island has not been diminished.

1. **"Nirvana"** -- home of William Gould Brokaw, off Beach Road, near Great Neck North High School, Nirvana Gardens.

2. **"Deepdale"** -- home of William K. Vanderbilt, Jr. Part of this estate is now the Lake Success Village Golf Club.

3. **"The Cove"** -- home of Mrs. Cord Meyer. This turn of the century mansion was demolished around 1950. Now the site is Cove Lane.

4. **"Bonnie Manse"** -- home of C. E. Finlay.

5. **"Sunshine"** -- home of H.S. Gilbert. Built around 1900, later owned by Harry Sinclair, and now the site of Sinclair Drive.

6. **"Martin Hall"** -- home of famed surgeon Preston Pope Satterwhite. Destroyed by a fire in 1932. Now the site of Martin Court. This 35-acre estate had formal gardens, garage & stable buildings, and 1,000 feet of water frontage on the Sound.

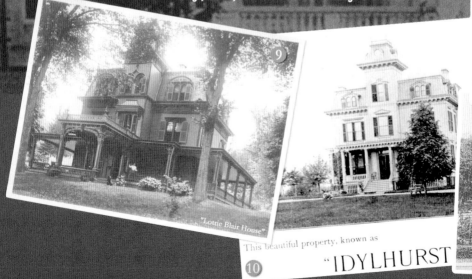

"Lottie Blair House"

This beautiful property, known as "IDYLHURST

⑩

"Nirvana"

7. **Walter P. Chrysler's Estate,** built around 1916 for Henri Bendel, is now part of the U.S. Merchant Marine Academy.

8. **E.C. Proctor** residence

"Deepdale"

9. **The Lottie Blair Parker House** was one of a handful of Victorian mansions along with Idylhurst.

"The Cove"

10. **Idylhurst,** Great Neck Estates, West side of Middle Neck Road

"Bonnie Manse"

"Martin Hall"

"Sunshine"

The Old Benjamin Hicks Residence, Great Neck

Mrs. H. P. Booth, Great Neck

...nce of Mr. E. J. Rickert, G

Walter Chrysler Estate, Kings Point Great Neck, L.I. N.Y.

Great Neck Train Station ca. 1920's, notice posting on station of "Luna Park" Coney Island.

I REMEMBER GREAT NECK.

One of our town's most colorful residents . . . the man wh

discovered W. C. Fields, Leon Erroll, Will Rogers and Eddie Cantor

. . . recalls a golden era when the world's great lived in Great Ne

By Gene Buck

Gene Buck

SALLY WON'T YOU COME BACK?
Words by GENE BUCK   Music by DAVE STAMPER

ZIEGFELD FOLLIES 1921
Lyrics by Gene Buck

Few people know it, but in the early days of Great Neck celebrities came from all over the world to attend fabulous house parties here, to talk over new books and plays, to catch opening nights at the *Playhouse.* The attraction was a star-spangled group of artists who were among the first to settle in Great Neck and to appreciate its unique beauty. This creative band, whose plays, novels, stage and screen roles were nationally known, helped put Great Neck on the map.

I recall one night when the bell rang at my home. At the door was a handsome young man. He bore a letter from a fine gentleman, Frank Crownshield, the editor of *Vanity Fair*. The letter read: " Dear Gene: This is to introduce a very good friend of mine who has come to live in Great Neck. Please make him feel at home. His name is F. Scott Fitzgerald." Fitzgerald's first book, "This Side of Paradise," was then a national sensation. It was only natural, therefore, for Fitzgerald to choose Great Neck to live in with his beautiful southern wife, Zelda. For Great Neck, after World War I, hummed with culture and creative personalities. People of the arts came here to live.

I came out to Great Neck in 1919, with my wife, Helen Faulkner. We were looking for a bit of country, not too much country, and accessibility to the city. We finally chose Great Neck because of its natural beauty and because we had some friends here. At the time I was Ziegfeld's writer, doing the lyrics for many of the "Follies." I was also Ziggy's talent scout. I spent nights haunting burlesque houses and vaudeville theaters.

The theater played a big part in Great Neck. Many of the foremost producers live here. Famous celebrities would come down for visits. Not far from where I now live, 69 Nassau Drive, Kennsington, Herbert Bayard Swope owned a house, right next door to Ring Lardner.

We used to have nice parties at my house. I had discovered W. C. Fields, Leon Errol, Will Rogers and Eddie Cantor and had put them in the Follies. They used to come down, as well as my song-writing friends. Victor Herbert would be here. He loved to eat. He'd eat anything. George Gershwin was another frequent house-guest. I still have a picture of George on my wall. Ziegfeld would often come down for the day. He liked to dance — ballroom dancing. He was one of the best waltzers I've ever seen.

It wasn't a wild town, no eccentrics. Most of the folks were home-loving. There'd be a great deal of talk, wonderful talk. And plenty of gags. Our parties were never formal. Theatrical people don't send invitations. They just get on the phone and soon there'd be a party. Vincent Youmans would come to my parties and he'd have a trick of singing and whistling his songs.

Author Ring Lardner used to come over and sing spirituals. He could play the piano a little. More than anything he wanted to become a songwriter. Later, I got him to write some of the sketches for the Follies. Lardner also put me in his stories. Used my real name, too.

A lot of work went on – Fitzgerald wrote "The Great Gatsby" in Great Neck, one of the finest short novels in American literature. Gatsby, if you recall from the recent film made from the book, was supposed to have been tied up with liquor-smugglers. Well, that's an interesting point. Since the North Shore was adjacent to the sea – and the rum-runners used to run boats in. Fitzgerald got to know a few of the bootleggers, and that's how he got the material for Gatsby. He was impressed by some of them, how they flashed $1,000 bills.

In what is now the Old Village, there was the *Playhouse*, where new shows were tried out. Everybody would come to town for them. There weren't any lights or phoney Hollywood glamour. Just real people who loved the theater.

The silent screen folk also had migrated to Great Neck. Thomas Meighan worked in Hollywood but lived in Great Neck. So did Richard Barthelmess. But then came talking pictures. As a result, many of our artists evacuated to Hollywood. Then, the depression hit. These two factors had the effect of dispersing Great Neck's theatrical colony.

Looking back, it was quite a fabulous era in American creative life, this colony where many lived and worked and played in such beautiful surroundings. It would be less than human for me not to look back without some bit of nostalgia. Yet, I've always felt that you can't live in the past. You must go forward. As I see it, the theatrical and literary folk saw the qualities of Great Neck. They discovered it --its unique character. An era of terrific development followed naturally.

Today, after looking back at my personal life here, I can't help feeling that Great Neck is still a unique community, geographically and pictorially.

Middle Neck Road ca. 1920's with grade crossing.

A Message from Joseph P. Day to the People of GREAT NECK and Vicinity

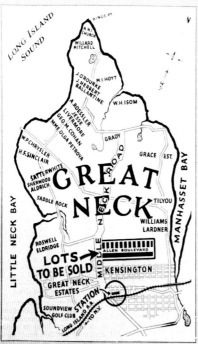

IMMEDIATELY after having read the statement published by Mr. I. G. Wolf in last week's issue of this newspaper I, personally, called on Mr. Frederick C. Gilsey, President of the Kensington Association, and on Dr. Theodore Sedlmayer, of North Drive, and discussed with them the outcome of the Allen Estate property Auction Sale on Saturday, May 16th.

In order to set their doubts at rest, I assured them that it is not, and never has been my practise to injure any neighborhood in which my organization held an auction sale; that it was our invariable custom to measure carefully the present character and future possibilities of a given locality and then, to do everything possible to sell the property to people of a class that would prove to be congenial and beneficial. Our work is Constructive and not Destructive. We aim to be Constructive Benefittors of a Neighborhood, and not Deteriorators.

I then stated that upon investigation I had found Kensington restricted to private dwellings on not less than four lots, and to cost not less than $8,500.

As the property known as the Allen Estate to be sold on May 16th is located just north of Kensington and diagonally opposite to Great Neck Estates—both of which are splendid residential sections richly deserving of protection—immediately conferred with the owners of the Allen Estate property who have restricted the residential section of their property, along the newly created Allen Boulevard and the streets adjacent thereto, as follows:

On Allen Boulevard, commencing 180 ft. East of Middle Neck Road, no dwelling excepting for private purposes, and costing not less than $8,500 and erected on a plot containing not less than 5,000 sq. ft., will be permitted to be erected.

Lots facing on the side streets, commencing on the East side of Day Court, will be so restricted that no house can be erected on less than 4,000 sq. ft. of plottage; shall be used for private dwelling purposes only; shall cost not less than $8,500, and shall be set back at least twenty (20) feet from the building line, exclusive of porches and piazzas, and shall not have what is commonly known as a flat roof.

These concessions and restrictions have brought great happiness and pleasure to Mr. Gilsey and Dr. Sedlmayer, both of whom are agreed that the forthcoming sale of the Allen Estate property, under these fair and reasonable conditions, will be beneficial to Great Neck, its property owners and residents, and not, in any way, harmful or deteriorating.

It is my very earnest desire that every resident of Great Neck shall feel the same way about it. To each and all I wish to offer my every assurance that you, your friends, associates and relatives, can attend the sale and buy as freely as if you, yourself, owned the property and were selling it, or conducting the sale. I want you to have the feeling that, in taking the time and trouble to attend the sale, you have at heart the best interest of the delightful community in which you live and, in mind, the higher future value of a property so well located and so desirable from every point of view. Your attendance at the sale and buying a plot or two, in my opinion, will be the best constructive work you can do, on Saturday, May 16th, for yourself, your children and your community.

Joseph P. Day

The Nine Villages

Nine areas of Great Neck incorporated as villages from 1911 to 1931. This was due to three reasons. First, Queens had been taken over by New York City just before the turn of the century. There were rumors that New York would soon absorb Great Neck. The residents of the peninsula decided that a more intimate government would best protect the rural, independent nature of their home. Second, there were also rumors of an imminent City of North Hempstead. Finally, Nassau County had only recently been established (1899), and was proving unable to cater to the rapidly growing peninsula's needs. Great Neckers wanted better roads, better sewer and trash management, better schools and better parks.

The first two villages to incorporate were Saddle Rock and Great Neck Estates in 1911. Kensington followed suit in 1917, and the Village of Great Neck and Kings Point did the same in 1922 and 1924, respectively. Lake Success incorporated in 1927, and Great Neck Plaza did so three years later. The last villages to join were Thomaston and Russell Gardens, both in 1931.

In order to do away with the problems, the incorporated villages issued strict building and zoning codes, and established intravillage governments.

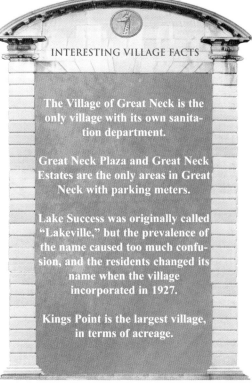

INTERESTING VILLAGE FACTS

The Village of Great Neck is the only village with its own sanitation department.

Great Neck Plaza and Great Neck Estates are the only areas in Great Neck with parking meters.

Lake Success was originally called "Lakeville," but the prevalence of the name caused too much confusion, and the residents changed its name when the village incorporated in 1927.

Kings Point is the largest village, in terms of acreage.

A horse and buggy at Kensington Gate

The intravillage governments generally controlled water, parks, and roads. After the formation of the Park District control of each village's parks was gradually handed over. They collect village taxes, and consist of a Mayor and a Board of Trustees. Mayors and Trustees serve varying terms and are nominally compensated for their duties. Mayors are responsible for preparing annual budgets, open for the public to see. Some villages have their own police forces. Nassau County's Police serve those that don't. Each village now has a planning board and a zoning board of appeals and an architectural review board.

The first major inter-village dispute occurred in the late 1920's. Dumping of trash had been outlawed in the Great Swamp (Kings Point Park), and disposal of garbage became a problem. No one wanted a landfill next door to them, and residents bickered their way to a standstill time and time again. In the end, the problem was solved with the construction of an incinerator in Garden City Park. The absence of a general Great Neck government was acknowledged to be a problem, and in 1929 Richard Schermerhorn published his plan for an inter-village government.

Today, the Village Officials Association, or VOA, is the inter-village forum Schermerhorn once outlined. It is part of the larger Nassau County Village Officials Association as well.

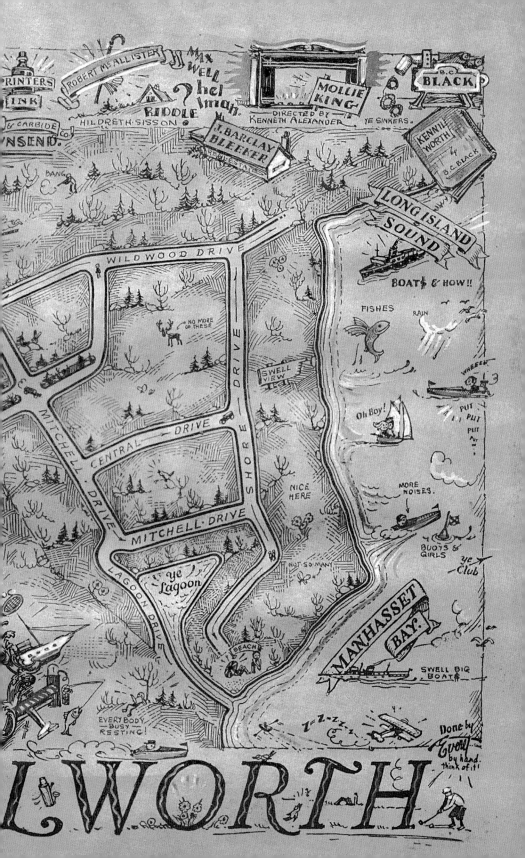

The Villages Then and Now

Village of Kings Point

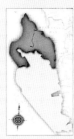

With 9 miles of picturesque waterfront and grand homes and estates on lots that are mostly one acre and larger, Kings Point is the golden tip of the Great Neck peninsula. The largest of the villages geographically, Kings Point is known for its meandering streets with tall trees and lush, manicured lawns and magnificent mansions. Backyard swimming pools and private tennis courts add to the village's opulent aura, though only a handful of large estates on more than two acres remain. Several neighborhoods within Kings Point, such as Kennilworth, Grace Harbor, Broadlawn Harbor and

Shelter Bay have their own pools and tennis courts. Some cul de sacs have a dock that they share. Wildwood Pool and Tennis Club, a private club, is located on Middle Neck Road in the village.

King Point Park, with 175 acres of woods, trails, playing fields and picnic grounds is owned by the village and leased to the Great Neck Park District. While the area is residential with about 1400 homes, the United States Merchant Marine Academy occupies 70 acres. Next to it, Steppingstone Park is owned by the Great Neck Park District.

Kings Point got its name from John Alsop King Jr., son of a governor of New York, who bought the estate at the northernmost tip of the peninsula from George Hewlett of the South Shore Hewletts, in 1851. It had earlier been called Haviland's Point and Hewlett's Point.

In the summer of 2001, a new village hall and police station opened at the corner of Kings Point Road and Steppingstone Lane, replacing the previous village hall that was housed in a Dutch Colonial that Walter Chrysler built for his daughter.

Children attend the John F. Kennedy Elementary School and the Great Neck North Middle and High Schools.

Village of Saddle Rock

With sweeping vistas of the Long Island Sound and New York City skyline, the village of Saddle Rock is a hilly community of private residential homes on the northwest shore of the Great Neck peninsula. Incorporated in 1911, it is the oldest and one of the smallest of the nine Great Neck peninsula villages. It got its name from a large saddle-shaped rock located just a few yards off shore in Little Neck Bay.

Children attend Saddle Rock

Elementary School and the Middle and North High Schools. The village is also in close walking distance to a number of houses of worship and the library.

Where the Eldridge mansion once stood, Saddle Rock's swimming pool, tennis and basketball courts, part of the extensive facilities of the village's private park facilities, now overlook the Grist Mill and Long Island Sound. There is also a bowls court, baseball field, badminton, volleyball, golf driving cage, putting area, and playground. Residents of Saddle Rock can also fish or set sail from the Village dock and mooring facility. A new Village Hall, dedicated in 1999, is also located at the park.

J. Leonard Samansky is running for his seventh term as mayor. Saddle Rock, he said, has 308 homes mostly on 1/3 acre lots. "Saddle Rock is a beautiful place to live and bring up a family," Mr. Samansky said. "We are the oldest village on the Great Neck peninsula and we have almost made it the youngest. We have improved our infrastructure." Strict zoning laws have scrupulously maintained the village's open airy views. The majority of homes are ranches built in the 1950's. Neither fences nor backyard swimming pools are allowed. Seven new homes are slated to be built on Saddle Rock's newest waterfront street, Bayport Lane North. Unlike Great Neck Estates, Harbor Hills or Kings Point, Saddle Rock also has sewers. "It's a valuable asset of the village," Mr. Samansky said.

Village of Great Neck

The Village of Great Neck, known as the "old village," is among Great Neck's earliest settlements and occupies 1.3 square miles. It has a population of 9,500 and is one of the more affordable areas of the peninsula. Though mostly single family tudors, capes, ranches, colonials and mediterranean homes, the village also has nine co-op apartment complexes and five rental buildings and is home to several synagogues, temples and churches. Plans are being discussed for the development of a condominium complex nearby and along the waterfront on East Shore

Road to replace the commercial areas. Along Middle Neck Road are numerous meat, fish and fruit markets, bakeries and other shops. Students who live in the village attend the Elizabeth M. Baker Elementary School and North Middle and High schools. The alternative Village School is also in the village along with Memorial Park and the Village Green.

Village of Kensington

Stately white pillars known as the Kensington Gates and a small park frame the entranceway to Kensington. A community of grand homes on broad streets to the east of Middle Neck Road, Kensington is walking distance to shopping, houses of worship and the train station.

With many historic homes, it was in many ways Great Neck's first residential community and the gates were a copy of London's Kensington Gates, from which the elegant community takes its name.

The developers, Charles Finlay, and

E.J. Rickert, built amenities that still grace its private park, such as a swimming pool and tennis courts, rare in the early 1900s. Their 150 homes sold for a whopping $15,000 to $35,000, at a time when no home north of the LIRR tracks sold for more than $4,000.

The neighborhood soon had a special cachet. Broadway stars, artists and socialites quickly moved in, including Flo Ziegfeld, Ed Wynne, P.G. Wodehouse, Herbert Bayarad Swope and Ring Lardner.

With a population of more than 1100, the village has its own police force. A private village park on East Shore Road has a pool and kiddie pool, tennis and basketball courts. The old Kensington-Johnson school house, which sat vacant for a number of years, has been replaced with a gated enclave of upscale condominiums and town homes. Children attend the Elizabeth M. Baker Elementary School and the South middle and high schools.

Village of Great Neck Estates

Hugging Little Neck Bay and the Queens border is Great Neck Estates, an elegant, tranquil village divided into gracious, older Tudor, Colonial and Mediterranean homes east of Bayview Avenue with more modern ranches and other estate-size villas on the waterside to the west, both laid out on curves and circles rather than a grid of streets. Among the smallest of the full service villages, Great Neck Estates has about 950 families and its own 13-member police force and public works department, all of the services of a much larger town in a very small pretty area. Centrally located, residents have easy walking access to synagogues, the main shopping district and the railroad. From the

stone promenade at the village's five-acre waterfront park the Manhattan skyline glistens in the distance. With a country club-type atmosphere, the park has a dock, mooring and launch service, adult and children's swimming pools, playground, playing fields, basketball and handball court and seven tennis courts, three enclosed in a bubble for the winter. An annual Memorial Day picnic is held for residents at the park, with an end of summer party on Labor Day. In the summer, the village operates its own day camp for vil-

lage children at the park. Part of Great Neck's commercial district along Middle Neck Road forms the village's eastern border, including about 70 stores and restaurants.

While generally an upscale village, including a Frank Lloyd Wright house, there are smaller homes on smaller plots in Great Neck Estates as well as two apartment buildings, one the Kenwood on Middle Neck Road and the other on the southern outskirts of the village. Even the village hall, located in an extensively renovated Dutch colonial, retains the area's ambience. Great Neck Estates has two wetland preserves, the Nature Preserve with a walking trail and Pond Park.

Village of Great Neck Plaza

What might be called Great Neck's Fifth Avenue, the Village of Great Neck Plaza is a charming town center with quaint brick sidewalks, antique-style lampposts, clocks and dozens of world class shops, boutiques, and restaurants within a lush suburban community.

"We are the hub of the Great Neck peninsula," said Jean Celender, the mayor of the pedestrian-friendly village. "While

we are an urban suburban downtown shopping district, it has a small town feel. You can go to a store and be on a first name basis with the merchants. "In fact, the Business Improvement's District's slogan is "Where everybody knows your name."

In the traffic island at the intersection of Middle Neck Road and Grace Avenue stands a 19th century clock, which is a replica design of the kind found in Winchester, England. The Plaza is New York City on Long Island with high end jewelry designers, shoe and pampering salons. The architecture includes prime examples of late 19th century commercial and residential buildings, pre-war 20th century apartment-hotels and an auto showroom, post-war garden apartments and several houses of worship. Unlike the rest of Great Neck, most residents in the Plaza are apartment dwellers. The village is in the process of landmarking historic buildings.

Great Neck Plaza is home to the peninsula's two hotels: the elegant Inn at Great Neck on Cutter Mill Road and The Andrew, a boutique hotel on North Station Plaza at Barstow Road. It was built in the 1960s and known until its recent avant garde renovation as the Bayberry-Great Neck Hotel.

During the 1960s, several nightclubs in the Plaza drew crowds to see celebrities such as Della Reese, as well as jazz players and Irish musicians. On Middle Neck Road, The Nightcap attracted a mixed clientele and was known as a "black and white bar." The Plaza still bubbles with activity. From the Squire movie theater to the numerous restaurants, it is still Great Neck's place to see and be seen.

The Plaza's Business Improvement District was established in 1989, the first BID established for a village municipality in New York State. Run by the Great Neck Plaza Management Council, it promotes the business district and holds an annual fall classic car show and street festival and a late spring sidewalk sale. There are informal gatherings, known as "Java with Jean" with Mayor Jean Celender and a summer lunchtime office concert series at various venues and a evening series of music and entertainment in the Grace Avenue Gazebo, Tuesdays at 8 p.m.

Village of Russell Gardens

What makes Russell Gardens special is its towering trees. Planted in the late 1920's and early 1930's, the trees form a canopy over all the streets in this .25 square mile village, one of the smallest in Great Neck. While it looks suburban, the village is only four blocks south of the Great Neck train station. And while it is close to shopping, the streets of Russell Gardens are quiet with a restful, rural feel. The village spends upwards of $50,000 a year to maintain the village trees by the sidewalks to maintain

the character of the village. All of the streets have sidewalks. Walking and running are popular activities. The close-knit community has an active civic association.

Along Northern Boulevard, Russell Gardens is home to Peter Luger's Restaurant, a renowned steakhouse. Within this charming village, laid out like an English Village, are 247 private homes, mainly English Tudors, French Normandy and split-level homes on quarter acre and smaller lots, along with a few farmhouses that date to the 1920's. There are also four apartment buildings, including one condominium. Daniel Berg Park is on Clent Road. Russell Gardens Association, a homeowner's group, maintains a pool, park and three clay tennis courts in a five acre park for residents to enjoy. Several office buildings line the commercial district along Northern Boulevard.

Russell Gardens was originally the old Schenck farm, later purchased by Captain Frederick Russell of Flushing. Eddie Cantor owned property where the park and pool now are and the composer Morton Gould lived here for a time. The actors W.C. Fields, Frederick March and Florence Eldridge lived in Russell Gardens.

Children attend Lakeville Elementary and the Great Neck South Middle and High schools.

Village of Thomaston

Built on Great Neck's highest hill, with a summit of 220 feet above sea level, the village of Thomaston is a quiet, charming, tree-lined community with distinct homes, some old, some quite modern, and a diversified population of artists and professionals that defies suburban stereotyping.

"When I first moved here, I remember that you could hear the quiet and we were just marveling how quiet, and then the ice

cream truck pulled up and rang its little bells and we fell in love with Thomaston," said Karen Epstein, a resident since 1984.

A quick walk to the train station, Thomaston lies north of Northern Boulevard and principally east of Middle Neck Road but is divided geographically by the railroad into northern and southern sections. Sixty percent of the village's 2600 residents live in single family homes; the rest occupy two family homes and apartment buildings, including two condominiums on South Middle Neck Road. Eighty percent own their own homes. Homes built in the late 19th and early 20th centuries line Susquehanna Avenue just north of Northern Blvd. Thomaston Park, one of two parks in Thomaston run by the Great Neck Park District, is also on Susquehanna Avenue.

There is also a small commercial area on East Shore Road.

Leila Mattson is the village historian. "After the LIRR provided a link from New York City to the Great Neck peninsula in 1899, the area began to be developed. Great Neck Hills and Great Neck Villa, two developments on the east side of Middle Neck Road, and Belgrave Square on the west side were combined to form the Village of Thomaston," Mattson said. "Thomaston, which is one square mile in area, was one of the last villages on the peninsula to be incorporated. In 1931 the new village, which took the name previously associated with the area around the railroad station, had a population of 250 residents. Population in the Village grew with additional developments."

"The Village has been named Tree City USA in honor of the towering trees which line Village streets. Village officials have been especially diligent in tending trees and actively replacing dying ones. In recent years the winding roads have been improved, and beautiful flower beds filled with a colorful variety of plants and thousands of tulip bulbs have appeared in many areas of the village. In 1990 village residents raised $15,000 to save a Chinese quince tree and have it moved from Schenck Ave. to the campus of Hofstra University," Mattson said.

Groucho Marx lived on Lincoln Road; Ray Charles on Schenck Avenue and the composer Morton Gould had a home on Shoreward Drive. Jane Cowl and Joseph Hirshhorn also lived in Thomaston.

The Great Neck Community School is on Schenck Avenue. The Great Neck Senior Center as well as two child care organizations, CLASP and Open Door, are located in the former elementary school building on Grace Avenue in Thomaston. Steak house row on Northern Boulevard has several of Long Island's best restaurants, including Morton's, Burton & Doyle and North Shore Steak House. With pointed

Victorian gothic windows filled with stained glass, the Korean United Methodist Church on Northern Boulevard, one of Thomaston's most prominent landmarks, was built in 1872. While the main church was destroyed by fire, the Victorian Sunday school and minister's house remain as reminders of a more rural era. The funds to build the church, parish house and parsonage came from Joseph S. Spinney, a commission merchant who lived on East Shore Road and commuted to Manhattan by steamboat.

Until well into the 20th century, much of Thomaston was considered part of Manhasset, with Manhasset Valley the center of activity in this rural area. Part of Thomaston joined the Manhasset school district and the southeastern tip of today's Thomaston is still in that district. The rest attend the Elizabeth M. Baker Elementary School and Great Neck South Middle and High Schools.

The Thomaston Village hall, dedicated in 1971, is a natural-colored split-face concrete block building on East Shore Road. Earlier village meetings were held in the firehouse on Prospect Street.

Village of Lake Success

There are more than 800 homes in Lake Success, the southernmost village on the peninsula where much of the land was once owned by the Vanderbilt and Phipps families. Earlier, the Matinecock Indians called it "Sucat Pond" and early settlers referred to it as "Suckess" when they built their first meeting house on the lake's shore.

Along Lake Success' winding, tree-lined streets are comfortable expanded ranch homes, split-levels, colonials, tudors and contemporary houses, many of which were built in the 1950s. As in other parts of Great Neck, many original homes have been knocked down and replaced with newer, grander dwellings. But it is golf for which Lake Success is known. The village sports an 18-hole residents-only golf course and a clubhouse. Residents can join the club for $1500 annually; there is a waiting list of several years for non-residents. The village also has an outdoor pool, playing fields and 11 tennis courts. Lake Success'

village hall and community center, built in the 1920s, were recently renovated but retain their Old World ambience and the sweeping views of Lake Success and the golf course. Additionally, the private Fresh Meadow Country Club also has an 18 hole golf course. Lake Success has its own police force. Kindergarteners through fifth graders attend Lakeville Elementary; middle and high school students attend the Great Neck South schools. The North Shore Hebrew Academy High School is also located in Lake Success. The Cumberland Adult Center offers an extensive array of courses, trips and special events.

The Unincorporated Areas

Several neighborhoods in Great Neck are unincorporated rather than part of the villages, though they have their own civic associations. Saddle Rock Estates, Harbor Hills, Allenwood, Upland, University Gardens and Lakeville are all residential areas where homeowners pay taxes and receive services such as street maintenance and zoning directly from the Town of North Hempstead rather than their own villages. Harbor Hills and University Gardens maintain their own pool and tennis courts.

I REMEMBER
GREAT NECK...

**The Man Who Has Sold More
Great Neck Acreage Than Anyone
Recalls Some Fabulous
Real Estate Deals**

by I. G. Wolf

As told to Enid Shevlin

Sulky-enthusiast Isaac Grover Wolf at the age of 20 with his black stallion Teddy R. at the entrance to Kensington Gates at extreme right.

My memories of Great Neck go back more than half a century, when there were only half a dozen buildings on Middle Neck Road from the Station to the Upper Village – a greenhouse, a couple of taverns and a few ramshackle houses. In 1891, when my family came here by steamboat, there were no lights on the main road and there were more horses in the center of town than in a Gene Autry western.

The biggest store in town was Nineslings (situated where Gilliar's Liquor Store is now) where one could get anything from a hammer to a haircut. More than once I waited with half a haircut while Old Man Ninesling took time out to sell a yard of calico! Up the road, next to Ed Smith's Meat Market (later sold to Fred Faigle) my father established his merchant tailoring business which he had brought out from New York.

We were brought to Great Neck by Mayor W. R. Grace, a customer of my father's, who persuaded the wealthy Merrit-Post families to let us have a twelve room homestead on eleven acres of ground, rent free. The house had long

stood idle and was supposed to be haunted. When, after three years, we could unfortunately report no ghosts.

Our rent was fixed at $25 per month and, after another three spookless years, raised to $35! When the owners finally jacked the rent up to $50, my family threatened to leave. Father was offered the house and all eleven acres for $11,000, no cash down, to be paid for in $1,000 worth of merchandise from his store per year. I've seen good buys in my years in Great Neck, but few to beat this, which, incidentally my father refused! The property was later sold to Frederick White for $75,000 and still later resold and cut up into building lots. The old house still stands, at 71 West Shore Road, now owned and occupied by Mr. Sam S. Levy.

My father, Abraham Wolf, was one of the pioneers who got things done in Great Neck. It was he and Richard Kehoe, a two-man committee, who won the battle for kerosene lamps on Middle Neck Road and went on from there to campaign for sidewalks and telephones

Great Neck was beginning to perk up! The telephone company agreed to install phones from the Station to All Saints Church if they could get fifty subscribers at $3.50 apiece. Some of these "first fifty" still have the same numbers allotted them half a century ago. The Kehoe Agency is still G. N. 1, Ziefman's Drug Store (now the Great Neck Pharmacy) is still listed as Great Neck 4 and I have the original Wolf's number, Great Neck 35.

Father, together with Kehoe and Judge Egbert LeCluse, who then owned a grocery store and Ed Crampton, owner of the livery stable on Hicks Lane, and a few other businessmen organized the Alert Fire Company, our first organization of volunteer fireman. Later, when Crampton became a contractor, a fast trip to Mineola Hospital in an Alert horse-driven hose cart saved his life after he had been badly injured by a dynamite blast. Throughout his life he was one of the staunchest supporters of the Alert Fire Dept.

As a result of all his civic activities, father soon progressed from the tailoring business to become Chairman of the Board of Assessors of the Town of North Hempstead. Later he started an insurance business in town which he carried on for fifty years. There were plenty of opportunities in those days for our ambitious pioneers!

When kerosene lamps were hung along Middle Neck Road, I was fascinated by our local lamplighter, Jacob Schmidt. He had his horse trained to zig-zag back and forth from one lamp to another, lighting them at dusk and dousing them at dawn, polishing chimneys, refilling the tanks and trimming the wicks – all for $150 per year. Do you know that West Shore Road and Bayview Ave. are still without lights? The estate owners there have always wanted to discourage traffic. As a result, in my day, this was the Lovers Lane of Great Neck.

Today, 95% of Great Neck's vast estates have been sold and developed into lots of one acre or more. I was instrumental in selling the William Gould Brokaw Estate for one million dollars, which became Nirvana Gardens, Strathmore, and the site of the present High School. In the lush twenties I sold and rented homes to some of the biggest stars in the theatrical world. I attended many of their fabulous parties at which entire Broadway shows were brought out for the entertainment of guests, I was the one who finally sold Eddie Cantor's white elephant home in Russell Gardens which he occupied only thirty days. When I built Tuscan Court, one of Great Neck's first three apartment houses, I had more money than brains!

There were fortunes to be made – and lost – in Great Neck real estate in the growing years, and I had my full share of the good and the bad. I still hold the record for selling the most expensive piece of business property in town, the northwest corner of Middle Neck at Cutter Mill Road, for $2,200 a front foot in 1928, the same property I had once sold for $50 a front foot! Fifty years ago the site of Harriette Ligety's store was worth $5,000; last year it sold for $85,000. As developer and part owner of Kenilworth, I saw water-front property sell as high as $100 a square foot, about twice as much as it brings today.

Across the years I've had a front row seat on Great Neck's changing scenes and, while it was rather sad to see the orchards vanish, the rolling farms disappear, and the vast estates broken up, that's the price we pay for progress. And after all, change and growth are the spice of life – especially to an old real estate man!

This is how they sold real estate 20 years ago. From an old advertisement. (as of 2003 that would be 70 years ago. Ed.)

DEPRESSION, WAR, AND THE UNITED NATIONS - 1929-1945

Old Swimming Beach - Steamboat Landing, now the Merchant Marine Academy - ca. 1934

1929-1945 - Depression, War and the United Nations

"Once in a while one of them cracks that it looks like they was bound to be a panic pretty soon and a big drop in prices, and so forth. This shows they're broad-minded and are giving a good deal of thought to up-to-date topics. Every so often one of them'll say: "The present situation can't keep up." The hell it can't!"

Finch, Ring Lardner's "The Big Town"

The Depression

Great Neck hit the Great Depression with a thud. Property values plummeted, forcing a number of people out of luxurious homes. Investors in Great Neck's development were simply hard to find.

Even I.G. Wolf's Tuscan Gardens Apartments on Middle Neck Road, painstakingly designed with old-style lamps and cobblestones fell victim to the crash and was lost to the mortgage company. Eddie Cantor had to sell his dream Tudor on 20-acres at Pine Hill and Lakeville roads due to the economic downturn.

School districts consolidated and teachers passed on their raises. The library passed on a number of books.

Great Neckers who were still relatively wealthy helped others through charities and other organizations. Meals and financial assistance were given to the needy. The ultimate goal, however, was to find work for every family. The Great Neck Emergency Relief Committee, the Great Neck Emergency Employment Committee and the Emergency Work Bureau helped citizens find jobs.

Great Neckers were not in terrible shape, however. A federal report showed that the average Great Neck resident spent over $500 (per year) more than the average American did. Then, as quickly as it had begun, the Depression was gone. Large estates that had been lost were subdivided to make room for smaller, moderately expensive homes. Great Neck was turning into a town of fairly wealthy people, and gradually becoming the community it is today.

The "Wedding Cake" building on the corner of Piccadilly Road and Middle Neck Road opened. Originally the ground floor of the building was an Oldsmobile showroom. Today, it is a courthouse.

Great Neck Record - 1930's Opening of "The Wedding Cake" building

The Merchant Marine Academy

The 82-acre campus has commanding views of the Throgs Neck and Whitestone Bridges and the Long Island Sound and is rich with history. Melville Hall, the Officers' Club, was named after Herman Melville, the author of Moby Dick and a Long Island resident. Once a summer residence for the silent movie actor Thomas Meighan, it was built around 1912.

The United States Merchant Marine Academy, the peninsula's only college, was established in Kings Point in 1938. The 1,000 midshipmen who attend the highly-selective federal service academy receive both military and academic training and live in dormitories on the former waterfront estate of automotive tycoon Walter P. Chrysler. Purchased by the U.S. Government in 1942, Chrysler's mansion is now the Administration Building, known as Wiley Hall. The midshipmen - 10 percent of whom are women -- dress in uniform and follow a rigorous and comprehensive curriculum, earning both a Bachelor of Science degree, a license as a merchant marine officer issued by the United States Coast Guard as well as an appointment as a commissioned officer in a reserve component of the U.S. Armed Forces. The Academy is also an NCAA Division III school offering 27 varsity sports to its midshipmen.

In 1979 the Museum opened to the public displaying America's maritime heritage. The original building was designed to resemble an Italian renaissance villa common to the Italian riviera.

Nearby is the Barstow house, the former home of William S. Barstow, an inventor of electrical devices at the turn of the century and an associate of Thomas Edison.

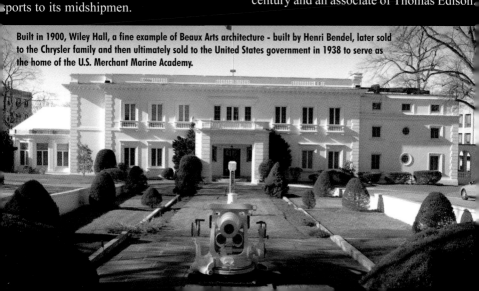

Built in 1900, Wiley Hall, a fine example of Beaux Arts architecture - built by Henri Bendel, later sold to the Chrysler family and then ultimately sold to the United States government in 1938 to serve as the home of the U.S. Merchant Marine Academy.

Built in the early 20th century, it is now the American Merchant Marine Museum, with a collection of old and rare navigational instruments. Ship models, including an 18-foot model of the famous passenger ship, SS Washington, paintings, prints and maritime artifacts illustrate the "Ships Made America" theme and tell the story of the tugboat industry. One gallery is dedicated to the wartime merchant marine; another to the academy itself.

Overlooking Long Island Sound.

Entering the great Wiley Hall, on view are the 20 - foot coffered ceilings and elegant balconies, as well as the original furniture used by the Chrysler family.

The Mariners Memorial Chapel is a national memorial honoring men of the Merchant Marine who gave their lives at sea during World Wars I and II in defense of their country. The site of many weddings, the chapel has a towering interfaith alter on an automatic turntable: its three sides corresponding to the Protestant, Catholic and Jewish faiths.

A beacon flashes at night from the Chapel's roof, visible for miles. It symbolizes the light that guides mariners lost at

The spectacular panoramic view of the Long Island Sound, featuring the NYC skyline in the far distance, as seen from the great terrace and lawn behind Wiley Hall and the Academy.

sea. A golden dome with a weathervane in the form of a full-rigged sailing ship tops the steeple.

Left and bottom: The Barstow house, now The American Merchant Marine Museum preserved many original features of one of the finest Gold Coast mansions. The music room still proudly features the wood carving and hand painted ceiling. Touring the Museum, one can view a great home and wonder just what it must have been like there overlooking Long Island Sound and the city beyond.

BVLGARI

diagono

World War II and the U.N.O.

Like most Americans during World War II, Great Neckers maintained a strong desire for neutrality until the bombing of Pearl Harbor on December 7, 1941. In fact, the head of the Woman's National Committee for Neutrality, Laura Megalls, resided on Station Road.

United Nations Headquarters, Lake Success. Built by the Sperry Gyroscope Company in 1941, the redesigned factory became the headquarters for the Security Council of the UN in August 1946.

Residents were not, however, inactive. People with and without families in Europe organized fundraisers and sent money and supplies overseas. The soon-to-be organization town was taking shape.

Wartime was marked by shows of patriotic sacrifice. The consumption of food and gas was cut significantly. People collected supplies such as scrap metal and rubber for their government.

William Wright was the first Great Necker drafted, and Edward Monroe Bates, Jr. the first to be killed. Bates Road is so named in his honor.

The United Nations Organization's first home was in what became the home of a series of military contractors, including the Sperry Gyroscope factory, in Lake Success.

Originally the newly minted organization had planned to meet at Hunter College,

NO KIDDING....ARE YOU REALLY DOING THE BEST YOU CAN, TOO ?.....

BUY EXTRA BONDS
4th WAR LOAN

The Gordon Shop
(Formerly Ninesling's)
629 MIDDLE NECK ROAD
Tel. Great Neck 134

but when their contract ran out in 1946, they turned to Great Neck. Some residents were not pleased.

Most residents were concerned about what the U.N.O.'s presence would do to Lake Success. While politicians assured the residents that their lives would not be disrupted, the final referendum vote was fairly close, with 102 residents voting for, 70 against the U.N.O.'s presence in Lake Success.

The first meeting of the Security Council took place in August in an unused portion of the factory. The building had been specifically renovated for the U.N.O.

While the Security Council met at their temporary location in Lake Success, the General Assembly congregated in Flushing Meadows. Many U.N.O. officials moved to Great Neck and became a part of the community. The LIRR accommodated the U.N.O. with a special train schedule. The January 1947 UN-GN Welcome Assembly was well attended, with 1,000 residents in the crowd.

When the organization moved to New York, many of the staff remained, becoming a part of the community for good. The flags of the permanent members of the Security Council still fly in front of the complex, but what became a giant weapons plant was renovated to accommodate office and warehouse space. The United Nations occupied the north building, a three story, 92,000 square foot office building, linked to the main building where submarines and airplanes were built. It was just part of the 1.4 million square foot complex on 94 acres. It was sold by Lockheed Martin for $21 million in 2000 to a partnership called I.park Lake Success.

The Great Neck Park District

Roswell Eldridge petitioned the Town of North Hempstead for the establishment of a Great Neck Park District in 1916, five months after the State of New York made such a district legal. The petition was approved, and the Great Neck Park District was formed.

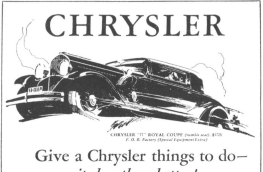

CHRYSLER

Give a Chrysler things to do— it does them better!

CHRYSLER "77" ROYAL COUPE (rumble seat), $1725
F. O. B. Factory (Special Equipment Extra)

Go through traffic in a Chrysler. Learn how nimbly and effortlessly it threads its way through the maze . . . how fast it is on pick-up . . . how easily it handles . . . how safe and sure are its weatherproof 4-wheel hydraulic brakes.

Take it out on the open road. Step on it . . . get the tingle of its speed . . . test its smoothness and quietness. Climb hills—

$795
NEW CHRYSLER SIX
Lowest-priced six ever to bear the Chrysler name. With such Chrysler engineering developments as weatherproof hydraulic brakes; 62-h.p. high-compression engine mounted on rubber; hydraulic shock absorbers; Chrysler-styled all-steel bodies. Five body styles, $795 to $845, f. o. b. factory

hills up which you have struggled laboriously in other cars. Watch the Chrysler pass everything on the steepest grades.

We will gladly place a Chrysler at your disposal so that you can give it things to do—difficult things—and learn for yourself how much better it does them than any other motor car that you have ever driven.

There is a Chrysler for every purse and need—Imperial, "77", "70", "66" and New Chrysler Six

Northern Boulevard Motor Sales Corp.

GREAT NECK, L. I.   *Telephone Imperial 2000*

Slowly, six villages — the Village of Great Neck, Great Neck Plaza, Kensington, Kings Point, Russell Gardens and Thomaston — joined the District. Great Neck Estates, Lake Success, and (interestingly, for the Eldridges ran) Saddle Rock declined to join the District. These villages supply their residents with exclusive use of village facilities.

The first meeting of the Board of Commissioners was held on August 31, 1916. The board consists of three commissioners serving three-year terms. Every year one term expires.

The first piece of land the Park District acquired was a public bathing beach at the westernmost end of Steamboat Road. The land was bought for $40,000. In the early 1920's Memorial Field, which was soon put to use by baseball and tennis players, was bought along with the Village Green. Part of the funds used to purchase the Village Green was $24.38 in pennies raised by schoolchildren.

The Green was bought from the Brokaws, and the present-day Park District building, the Great Neck House, is on that property. The building was purchased in 1974.

Later in the 1920's, Allenwood Park, also used for baseball and tennis, was created. All three parks from the 1920's have added children's playgrounds.

Kings Point Park was established during the Great Depression; its construction employed over 150 out of work individuals. In 1938, the Village of Kings Point agreed to lease the 175-acre plot (mostly made up of what was called "the Great Swamp") to the District in exchange for a promise that the land would be serviced and improved. Nowadays, Kings Point Park teems with activity year-round, offering bike and nature trails, baseball and softball fields, tennis courts, soccer fields, picnic areas with grills, a sled hill, and cross country ski trails.

The Park District expanded further in 1941, securing the Cutter Mill, Grace Avenue, and Wyngate Parks. These parks do not have ball fields. They have children's playgrounds with slides and swings and water spouting sculptures for summertime fun and grass for calm relaxation. Concerts are held weekly at the gazebo at the Jonathan L. Ielpi Firefighters' Park.

The United States Government bought the original public bathing beach in 1942 in order to create the Merchant Marine Academy. As a replacement, the Park District purchased Steppingstone Park and Marina, which now features a fishing float, a 284-foot dock, a wading pool, indoor and outdoor playgrounds, picnic tables, gardens and a snack bar. During the summer, outdoor concerts and shows are held on the waterfront stage every weekend.

In 1964, the Parkwood Complex opened. It boasted an Olympic-size outdoor swimming pool and smaller children's pools, an ice-skating rink with a fireplace and snack bar. In 1970 the rink was enclosed, enabling year-round use. Besides children's lessons, adult skating lessons are offered on a variety of days and times, including evenings at the Parkwood Rink.

A hockey skating program for younger children is a prerequisite to the ice hockey program, which includes team play.

During the off-season, the Parkwood rink is also used for inline skating. Hundreds of Great Neck children started taking lessons, learned to twirl and glide on the ice at the Parkwood rink. At age 3, a girl named Sarah Hughes from Kings Point, wanting to be able to skate like her older siblings, started taking lessons at Parkwood. Soon she was gliding across the rink and spinning with grace and ease. In 2002, Sarah, then 16-years-old, won the Olympic gold medal.

Outdoor tennis courts and a four-court indoor tennis complex were later added to the Parkwood Complex, with lessons, court time and camp programs available for young and old.

The Park District owns the commuter parking lots near the train station. Residents within the district can purchased a permit sticker in advance and pay a monthly or daily fee to park. The lots are not open to non-residents.

The Park District controls 21 parks and a number of parking lots. It is another Eldridge innovation that changed the face of Great Neck forever.

Skaters at Parkwood ice rink

A Look at The Parks

Memorial Field on Fairview Avenue (773-3420) bustles with activity. It is here that children and adults play soccer, baseball, basketball and tennis. Also known as the Athletic Field, this flat, open park in the Old Village has 16 Har-Tru tennis courts, softball and baseball diamonds, soccer fields, handball and basketball courts and a children's playground and bathroom facilities. The Great Neck P.A.L. is headquartered in a new building at one end. The park is open until dusk in the summer. The tennis courts open; weather permitting, on or about May 1. Eight courts close on or about Nov. 20 and the remaining eight close on or about Dec. 15, or the first freeze. Weather permitting; the courts are open from 9 a.m. to dark. Tennis permits are required from June 1 through September 30 at all Park District tennis courts.

The largest of Great Neck's parks, **Kings Point Park**, with entrances at Steamboat Road and Redbrook Road (482-9257) is a woodsy paradise spread over 175 acres. There are more than five miles of trails for hiking and cross-country skiing and picnic areas with tables and outdoor grills. It also includes 4 softball diamonds, 4 Har-Tru tennis courts, 2 all-weather basketball courts, a soccer field, horseshoe pitching. The park's sled hill is a popular spot on snowy winter days. The park has restrooms facilities. The tennis courts are open on or about May 15 and close on or about Oct. 15. Weather permitting, in full season, the courts are open from 8 a.m. – 8 p.m. Tennis permits are required from June 1 through September 30.

Tucked at the corner of Kensington, lush with towering trees is **Allenwood Park**, on Allenwood Road. (487-4360). With a duck pond, pheasants, rabbits, fanciful play areas and aqua park with animal sculptures spouting and sprinkling water,

it's a favorite spot for the wee ones, especially when the ice cream trucks drive past and ring their bells. Allenwood's facilities also include softball diamonds, 5 all weather tennis courts and a basketball court. The tennis courts are open year round from 9 a.m. to dusk.

The gazebo at the Village Green.

The **Village Green** in the center of the Village of Great Neck on Middle Neck Road retains the aura of an old-fashioned park; its benches provide a welcome respite on a sunny afternoon. (482-0181) Here is Great Neck's Veterans' Memorial, as well

The Veterans Memorial wall at the Village Green.

as a formal rose garden, gazebo, a bandstand for concerts, a senior exercise course and a children's playground.

Spectacular views of the Long Island Sound make **Steppingstone Park** on Steppingstone Lane in Kings Point (487-

9228) the most visually dramatic of Great Neck's parks. A valid park card is required to enter the park, which has a marina with mooring facilities, a dock and a boat launching ramp. Here Park District Residents can take sailing lessons through the Steppingstone Sailing School or fish from the dock.

But the fun is not just by the water. Steppingstone has a colorful indoor playground that delights the youngest residents and an imaginative outdoor children's playground with a big, red replica of a boat for young sailors to explore. There's a wading pool, aqua park with animal shaped sprinklers, snack shop and picnic tables on a hilly slope. The Steppingstone Waterside Theatre draws a big crowd for its musical and theatrical programs weekends, evenings and holidays.

At **Uplands Park**, at Bates and Soundview Rd, there are basketball and handball courts, a children's playground, shade trees, benches and a child-sized train.

Thomaston Park on Susquehanna Avenue is a good spot to pick up a basketball game. The neighborhood park also has sitting areas, horseshoe pits, checkers/chess tables, a children's playground and a gazebo.

Cutter Mill Park, along Great Neck Road (829-5428) also offers a water-spouting aqua park for play on hot summer days, a children's playground, picnic tables, basketball court and a children's playground.

Facing Manhasset Bay on Ravine Road, **Ravine Park** has shady trees, benches, a children's playground and a miniature gazebo.

Lakeville Park on Pembroke Ave (482-9502) offers restrooms, basketball courts, children's playground and an aqua park. Near the main post office, **Wyngate Park**, at the intersection of Wyngate and Shoreward Drive, has two play areas and basketball courts.

The newly renamed Jonathan L. Ielpi firefighters park.

Manor Park on Cumberland Ave has a children's playground, aqua park and tables along with restroom facilities.

Jonathan L. Ielpi Firefighters' Park, formerly the Grace Ave. Park on Grace Ave. (829-2691) offers respite just a quick stroll from the bustle of Middle Neck Road in Great Neck Plaza. A popular spot for young and old alike, the park has a grand gazebo where live performances are held on summer evenings. To the other side are a brightly-hued children's playground with swings, slides and an animal-themed aqua park. Grace Avenue Park also has picnic tables and restroom facilities.

The three passive parks within the park district don't offer recreational facilities but are the perfect spot for reflection and strolling. These quiet, natural, wildlife preserves are Creek Park (Daniel Jay Berg Memorial) on Great Neck Road; Wooleys Lane Park, on Wooleys Lane; Udalls Pond Park by the main library and the Woodland Preserve, on Beach Road.

The villages of Lake Success, Great Neck Estates, Kensington and Saddle Rock have private park facilities with swimming pools, tennis courts and other amenities for their residents. Unincorporated areas such as Harbor Hills and the neighborhoods of University Gardens, Broadlawn Harbor, Grace Harbor, Shelter Bay and Kennilworth also have private recreational facilities for use by their residents.

THE PENINSULA GOES GLOBAL
1945-2002

For Men Only.

A Feature About Great Neck Women .... To Be Read By Their Husbands

Do you think your wife spends too much on her wardrobe? Here's the result of a door-to-door survey made last month by CIRCLE MAGAZINE reporters of the buying habits of 500 housewives residing in Kings Point, Kensington, Kennilworth, University Gardens, Russell Gardens and the Estates. Suggestion: if your wife is under average, tear out this page before passing on the issue.

- The average Great Neck housewife has six charge accounts.

- She purchases a minimum of 16 dresses and suits a year. (More if she travels south for the winter or takes a cruise.)

- She buys eight bottles of cologne a year, two bottles of perfume.

- She spends approximately $350 a year on negligees, underwear and hosiery.

- She visits the beauty parlor 1 ½ times a week

- 72% drive their own car.

- She buys eight pocketbooks a year, ten hats, from 11-16 pairs of shoes.

- She spends about $250.00 a year on costume jewelry, compacts and trinkets.

- 81% have their own checking account, 19% share a joint account with their husbands.

Originally Published GREAT NECK CIRCLE MAGAZINE 1951

The Peninsula Goes Global - 1945-2002

1945-1960: A Classic Suburb

Great Neck entered the postwar era energized and ready to stretch its legs. A relatively dormant real estate market awoke, and houses and apartment buildings appeared in numbers never before seen. Over 40% of present-day Great Neck's housing was completed in the period from the end of the war to 1960.

Developers set to work creating communities. When space to build entire communities became scarce, developers began buying single-home properties and splitting them into halves, thirds, and quarters.

People wanted to buy the new houses faster than they were built. The very day a development of houses on Baker Hill went on the market every home was sold. In the Village of Great Neck alone, the population went from 6,200 in 1940 to 10,100 in 1960.

When the developers ran out of plots to split, they attempted to construct apartment buildings. In April of 1949, Great Neck Towers opened its doors. The Kensington Gate Apartments were constructed. A seemingly endless flow of people poured into what was once a tiny farming town. Property was getting more valuable by the day.

In 1951 Sol Atlas built the North Shore Mart, a shopping center focused around Wanamaker's Dept. Store where "The Gardens at Great Neck" anchored by Waldbaum's now stands. Originally Atlas, also the developer known for bringing the finest Fifth Avenue shops to Long Island with the Miracle Mile in Manhasset, built a beautiful garden, replete with trees and other greenery to decorate his model shopping center. This assembly of flora is known today as the parking lot.

Not all of the growth was welcomed. Great Neckers had been on their guard for over 30 years when the apartments start-

Dwight D. Eisenhower parade Middle Neck Road ca. 1951

ed appearing. The veteran residents did all they could to stop construction of the massive, rectangular blocks that urbanized the once-rural town. When they couldn't stop

John Wanamaker Dept. Store was the original anchor at "The Gardens" and featured a grand staircase. Now it houses a billiards hall, North Shore Fitness Club and Waldbaums. John Wanamaker New York, selected Great Neck as the site for their first surburban branch store.

United States Post Office in Great Neck. Limestone Art Deco-style building which stands at the intersection of Welwyn Road and Shoreward Drive.

the building they forced other restrictions on the developers, such as compulsory gardens or height restrictions on buildings, as were the cases with the Kensington Gate Apartments and Great Neck Plaza, respectively. Store owners feared that the North Shore Mart would cause shoppers to abandon Middle Neck Road stores, rather than, as it panned out, bring more customers to Great Neck.

The Village of Lake Success purchased the Deepdale Country Club in order to prevent the land from being developed.

Aerial photo of Kensington.

Russell Gardens wrestled with the descendents of Captain Frederick Russell over whether or not they could make commercial use of their property.

The Great Neck Circle magazine chronicled this era. An article on *Gentleman Farmers of Great Neck* for instance, appeared in the fall of 1952. "There's more to Great Neck than Cadillacs and convertibles, swimming pools and supermarkets, traffic jams and train schedules," wrote Enid Shevlin. "A short fifteen-minute drive from the station, you can see sheep grazing on the western side of the peninsula and a herd of contented cows on its eastern slope."

The livestock belonged to Wall Street broker Manuel Weisbuch, who bought ten acres of the Gignoux farm along with a prize herd of two dozen pure bred Jersey cows, and obtained grazing rights on 150 acres still owned by Gerard Gignoux plus 10 more acres for raising fodder corn. The cows produced about 200 quarts of creamy raw milk daily at the Minnamere farm between East Shore Road and the Sound. Great Neck's first school house is still on the property, later the first fire hall in town.

On the western side of Kings Point, Mr. and Mrs. Grean, she noted, kept sheep grazing on their front lawn of their New England-style farmhouse, raised pullets and capons and all their own vegetables and fruits on the two-acre property.

"By turning their own flock of ten sheep loose on their lawn, the Greans have dispensed with both lawn mowers and fertilizers, using only shepherd's crooks to keep the animals away from rose bushes which they relish as much as the crab grass. Neighbors frequently borrow the flock to beautify their own lawns," Shevlin noted.

When the Village of Great Neck Plaza passed a landmark ordinance in 1978 and the Grace Building at 11 Middle Neck Road was added to the National Register of Historic Places, a large sculpture of a jester was placed on the corner building to celebrate. It added to the village's new prominence. The Jester was sculptured by Howard Goldberg.

1960-Present: Religion and Diversity in Great Neck

In recent years Great Neck has become increasingly diverse. Among the residents are Hispanic, Chinese, Indian, Israeli, Iranian, Japanese, Koreans, South African and African Americans. This is especially evident in the wide range of houses of worship on the peninsula.

"I see it as a night scene by El Greco: a hundred houses, at once conventional and grotesque, crouching under a sullen, overhanging sky and a lustreless moon."
Nick Carraway, F. Scott Fitzgerald's The Great Gatsby

F. Scott Fitzgerald's Nick Carraway sees Great Neck as a godless place. He could not be more wrong. There are over 25 houses of worship in Great Neck. Many others are in the works. Great Neck is blessed with different Protestant denominations, a Catholic church, Reform, Conservative, Orthodox and Sephardic Jewish congregations and more.

What is now the Village School, the alternative public high school, was first the free, multi-denominational Union Chapel

All Saints Church

built on Henry Allen's land. The building, erected in 1863, lasted as a house of worship for 23 years. In 1886, it gave way to a more spacious structure, the Episcopalian

St. Aloysius

All Saints Church, on northern Middle Neck Road, at the edge of Kings Point. Great Neck's wealthiest, most active families, the Eldridges, Gignouxs, Kings, Messengers, Morgans, and Hewletts collaborated to create a charming old-fashioned stone church with stained glass windows. In fact, the architects of Saint Patrick's Cathedral in New York City were entrusted to design it. Here the annual Blessing of the Animals and Strawberry Festival is held. Bishop Littlejohn, the first Bishop of Long Island, is buried in All Saints Cemetery.

According to Episcopalian law, only a congregation that has met for a year can build its own church. Therefore, for the final year before All Saints' construction the Episcopalians had exclusive use of the Union Chapel. The other religious groups were forced to find other places to worship for the year, and each went its separate way.

St Paul's Episcopal Church

Top Left:
Community
Church and
Temple
Isaiah

Top Right:
Temple
Beth El, the
first and
largest
synagogue in
Great Neck.

The independence from the Chapel worked its magic, and by the time their displacement was over, none of the religious groups wanted to come back to the Union Chapel.

Joseph Spinney, for whom the Spinney Hill area is named, founded the United Methodist Church in 1872. Catholics found salvation from a weekly trek to Flushing in 1876, when St. Aloysius Roman Catholic Church was built. The present stone structures were finished in 1913, but the church's parochial school closed down several years ago due to dwindling enrollment.

Bond Street's Community Church was founded in 1914 and completed in 1925. Later, this church provided sanctuary to Temple Beth El (1928-1932), Temple Emanuel (1960's), and the NAACP. Temple Isaiah, now located in the Community

a Hebrew school and is moving to Chelsea Place. Ted Tsuruoka is the rabbi.

In 1924 what later became St. Paul's Episcopal Church on Grace Avenue separated from All Saints to form its own congregation and building. St. Paul AME Zion Church and Bethel Baptist church both opened on Steamboat Road in the 1930's. Along with Spinney Hill, this area has long been home to many African Americans. In

Bottom Left:
Temple
Emanuel

Bottom Right:
Great Neck's
first Torah
dedicated to
Temple Beth
El by Abram
Wolf, in mem-
ory of his wife
Rose. Courtesy
of the Elsie K.
Rudin Judaica
Museum of
Temple
Beth El

Church of Great Neck, was founded by members of Temple Emanuel in 1967. The smallest of the Reform temples, it also has

1953, North Shore Presbyterian Church on Lakeville Road was formed.

The Korean Presbyterian Church briefly used the North Shore Presbyterian Church's facilities in the eighties, and a Korean Apostolate was formed as part of St. Aloysius. The Christian Science Church (founded 1929) recently experienced a makeover at the hands of Brahma Kumaris, and the South Middle Neck Road building is now the home of the Global Harmony House.

Temple Beth-El, a Reform congregation, was the first Jewish house of worship in Great Neck. Opened in 1928, it was the first of three synagogues to be built on Old Mill Road. The original edifice was designed to blend in architecturally with the community and the Tudor style sanctuary in the chapel bears some resemblance to All Saints, as both congregations worship within houses of stone and stained glass. At Beth El's inception, Great Neck had a Jewish population of just 115 families and a general population of 12,000 people. The Wolf family, the first Jewish family in town and founding members of the temple, donated one of the first Torah scrolls in 1929.

Temple Beth El's original building has been enlarged three times during the past 65 years. A dramatic, contemporary sanctuary was added in 1970, with a soaring white interior and lots of light, and a Aeolian Skinner Pipe Organ with more than 3200 pipes. The sculptor Louise Nevelson created the *Bima* or alta wall and the Ark and Eternal Light. Its carved forms are a Holocaust memorial entitled "The White Flame of The Six Million." Today, the reform congregation, under the leadership of Rabbi Jerome K. Davidson, boasts a 1,250 family membership. In May, 2001, a fire left all but the sanctuary unusable. A new school, offices and meeting rooms are being built and the rest of the facilities renovated and renewed. The Rabbi Jacob Rudin Chapel is named for its first spiritu-

al leader. Rabbi Rudin served the congregation for four decades.

Temple Israel, the leading Conservative Jewish congregation on Long Island, was founded in 1940. Temple Israel quickly outgrew its original sanctuary for 100 members in a house on Preston Road. In 1949, the congregation built a large com-

Temple Israel

plex on Old Mill Road. The main sanctuary is in a colonial style two-story red brick building with a four columned entryway. The newly renovated temple now serves 1,300 families, with a religious school, Beth HaGan Nursery School and extensive

Rabbi Mordecai Waxman

ballroom and catering facilities. The Waxman High School and Youth House is located in a separate building at the rear of the property. The temple's Senior Mitzvah Group meets twice weekly with classes and cultural activities geared specifically to seniors. The late Rabbi Mordecai Waxman, a major force in shaping the local Jewish community, setting standards in the Conservative movement and in improving relations between Catholics and Jews worldwide, led the congregation for 55 years.

The peninsula's postwar Jewish population boomed, and Temple Emanuel separated from Beth El in 1953 (as Beth El had capped its membership), becoming Great

Neck's second Reform synagogue. Their building, dedicated in 1959 and recently enlarged, is located at Hicks Lane, at the gateway to Kings Point. The Hebrew school and nursery school were recently expanded and renovated, complemented by expansive ballroom and catering facilities. It has a meditation garden in the back with a large bronze menorah and an art gallery in the hallway leading to the lobby. Above the ark in the sanctuary is a Torah scroll from Czechoslovakia that survived the Holocaust. The scroll is open to the Ten Commandments. Stained glass windows flank the ark. Rabbi Robert S. Widom leads the congregation.

Situated at the westernmost edge of Nassau County, Great Neck was the first major draw to city dwellers looking east for homes and property after World War II. The Jewish community became known for its vitality, its richness in programming, and in terms of children receiving a Jewish education. With so many other draws – fine public schools, parks and an easy commute to the city – it became the preeminent Jewish community on Long Island. With so much to offer, it was easily affordable and a place for young families to aspire to. And as a vital Jewish community, Great Neck has produced national leadership in the American Jewish community on many levels.

The Lake Success Jewish Center

In 1962, the Lake Success Jewish Center, a Conservative temple was established on a woodsy, four-acre plot on Lakeville Road.

The Great Neck Synagogue

The Great Neck Synagogue, an Orthodox congregation with a sanctuary designed in the round, with women sitting in tiered rows above the men's section, was founded in 1951. The congregation first met on the last day of Passover that year in a rented space above the Squire Theatre. Herman Wouk, the bestselling author of *The Caine Mutiny* and *The Winds of War* and a resident of Kings Point at the time, was a founding member and chanted the festival service.

A few years later the congregation moved into an old gray frame house at 26 Old Mill Road, next to the Great Neck Women's Club. As the synagogue flourished under the leadership of now retired Rabbi Dr. Ephraim Wolf, a new synagogue, gymnasium and the original building of the North Shore Hebrew Academy were built on the four-acre property. Among the early members of the Great Neck Synagogue was Richard Tucker, the famed Metropolitan Opera tenor, who sang the concluding song at Saturday morning services.

The thriving congregation now has 570 families under the spiritual leadership of

North Shore Sephardic Synagogue

Rabbi Dale Polakoff and bustles with activity every Sabbath. A new youth center was recently constructed. As the home of the North Shore Mikveh Association, the synagogue also houses a ritual bath, the only one on the North Shore of Long Island.

Young Israel of Great Neck

In recent years, the Orthodox population of Great Neck has grown rapidly. Young Israel of Great Neck was established to meet the needs of an ever-growing community in 1974. The synagogue built their sanctuary where the North Shore

Beth Hadassah Synagogue

Community Arts Center once stood and later expanded into a former bank building

Mashadi Jewish Center

next door. Rabbi Yaacov Lerner has led the congregation since its inception.

Great Neck's Persian population has grown dramatically since the 1970's and in recent years numerous Sephardic synagogues have been erected and organizations started. The Persian community is split between the Mashadis and Tehranis, each with their own customs and synagogues. The Iranian Jewish Center, a Tehrani congregation also known as Beth Hadassah Synagogue, was built in 1993 on the site of a former tennis court. Just a few hundred feet down Steamboat Road, the Mashadi Jewish Center opened a little later. Also in 1993, Beth HaKnesset Ahavat Shalom, the double-domed North Shore Sephardic Synagogue, was established on Cutter Mill Road.

Chabad of Great Neck, an Orthodox Jewish congregation, opened its doors in 1995, inviting those who wanted to worship at the former Bender Estate overlooking Manhasset Bay in Kings Point to its sanctuary. The Lubavitch group has filed for permission to build a new synagogue and day school on the property.

Inside the Cherry Lane campus of the North Shore Hebrew Academy in Kings Point is the sanctuary of the Cherry Lane Minyan, an Orthodox synagogue under the direction of Rabbi Marvin Tokayer, one of the world's foremost authorities on Jews in the Far East. The Cherry Lane Minyan is unique in Great Neck and in world Jewry. Half the members are Ashkenazic Jews; half are Persian or from

Share Zion

Sephardic backgrounds. As a result, tunes from both strains of Judaism are used in the synagogue.

Other synagogues have sprung up over the years, as well, including the Syrian synagogue, Share Zion, built from Jerusalem stone where a medical building once stood on Middle Neck Road. An Iraqi congregation meets in a new Babylonian Synagogue on Great Neck Road that was once a vacant commercial space. Several stores and restaurant serve as synagogues on Saturdays,

Babylonian Synagogue

as well. And in response to the growing number of traditional and observant Jews, numerous kosher shops and restaurants have opened in town.

On Saturdays, crowds walk to synagogue. Kebabs with rice, kosher Chinese food, kosher steakhouses plus several kosher pizza and sushi shops are now as familiar as the Ashkenazi fare of corned beef on rye and bagels with cream cheese.

On most days, the bells of All Saints Church can be heard at the tip of Kings Point. One of Great Neck's most attractive points is the vast array of religious institutions available. Great Neckers are deeply involved in their houses of worship. Much like their predecessors here, they have thrived on the opportunity to worship freely. They have grabbed religion (as they have most other aspects of life) by the horns and created vibrant religious communities.

Voices of Great Neck: Rabbi Jerome K. Davidson

Rabbi Jerome K. Davidson

I first arrived here in 1958. By the time I came, it was a strongly Jewish community, but I would imagine that percentage has doubled. It might have been 25-30 percent or more and now it's 65 percent or more. A sizable Protestant community has more or less moved away, a significant Persian community has come in and an Asian community has come in and then, in terms of demographics, the Orthodox community has become larger as well than it was. Particularly on Saturday they are more visible."

"It's a very vital, politically, intellectually active community, liberal in its general spirit and a very open kind of community with a lot of vitality. Almost all of its institutions are exemplary for whatever they do, whether it's the UCF or COPAY or the senior citizens community organizations or after school groups, the synagogues — they are all rather extraordinary. It's a high quality community. I never cease to be amazed when I meet with the children in our synagogue, how bright and connected to the world they are. The generations of adults in the community are similarly exceptional people."

"When I talk to people who come here, they come for the schools. They come for the strong sense of community. It's not like living in some suburbs where you don't know where one ends and the next begins. Here in Great Neck you have a real base and a sense of cohesiveness. Basically the parks and the schools are unifying elements in the community. You have a sense of community. It's an easy commute yet a beautiful place to live."

"The environment differs from many other suburbs: it has so many opportunities for participation on many levels -- music, and the arts, intellectual activities in the library or other groups. Adult education is an amazing institution in and of itself."

"The villages, even though there are so many of them and they have their own agendas, will come together and really work together for common issues. There are diverse points of view in the community, of course, but that's what makes it a healthy place. But it's a highly intellectual, politically active, vibrant place."

"Great Neck is a very stimulating place. Older people who have moved here from somewhere else are taken by surprise at all there is to offer and they really thrive in it. You'd have to look pretty far and wide to find a community that has this much to offer. It's a fine community. Most of the people who have moved here in recent years are very happy that they did."

Voices of Great Neck:
Monsignor Brendan P. Riordan

Monsignor Brendan P. Riordan

St. Aloysius Parish was founded in 1876. In 1976, we began our 100th year anniversary as a Catholic parish. A wooden Gothic-style Church served the people very well until 1912. To serve an ever-growing population, the new Byzantine Romanesque-style church was built. It must have looked like St. Peter's Basillica in the sleepy little town that Great Neck was."

"St. Aloysius could never be repeated. The artisans used...the amount of money... the church will last forever."

"As time went on with the growing Jewish population here in Great Neck, it's a misnomer that there aren't any Christians in Great Neck. Actually there are 1,400 families registered and 1,000 people who attend mass here every week. It's a very, very viable parish."

St. Aloysius

computer school, and religious education. We have a large Korean and Hispanic community with special ethnic celebrations."

"We are very proud of our ethnic diversity and having two different religions working together in the same building. For the last two years, Temple Beth El had no place to go when the hebrew school burned. We are the first to share the school."

"The classroom with the crucifix has a Star of David, and a *mezuzah* on the door. Everyone gets along just fine. Much to everyone's surprise, the Jewish kids are learning about Christianity and the Catholic kids are learning about Judaism. It's actually very nice."

"We are most proud of our outreach program; we are doing a great amount for the hidden poor. This is one community that doesn't like to admit that there are poor people. We help newly arrived immigrants with different skills, moving them from entry level jobs into jobs with good resumes. Professional people in the mainstream, very interested in education, no handouts from the government. It's a very dynamic thing to see. These are going to be great Americans."

"Many people consider St. Aloysius to be one of the most beautiful churches on Long Island. St. Aloysius is a church for those who continue to consider it home and for those who are seeking to return home."

"The school was founded in 1923, but in 1990, the building was renovated for outreach programs, sports programs, CYO,

Great Neck Schools: A Top-notch Education

Great Neck High School, during construction. William A. Derbusse, Jr. Inc. Contractor

"We moved here because...we wanted a quiet place, hygienic, with a good school, preferably public, and good air. We got it all."
-- Will Durant, Historian and Great Neck Parent, 1936

Great Neck, as a youthful, vibrant community, has taken pride in its commitment to education for years. Great Neck is home to two of the nation's best public high schools, a stellar Adult Education program, Jewish day schools and many other centers of learning.

The Great Neck Union Free School District services Great Neck, North New Hyde Park and part of Manhasset Hills, with more than 5,900 pupils enrolled in Kindergarten through grade 12. Students come from over 40 countries.

The Elizabeth M. Baker, John F. Kennedy, Lakeville and Saddle Rock are the district's elementary schools. Class sizes are limited with both gifted and enrichment programs. From those four schools students continue to either the Richard S. Sherman Great Neck North Middle School or the Great Neck South Middle School, depending primarily on where the pupil lives. About 130 attend an early childhood development center based on financial need.

The John L. Miller Great Neck North High School has consistently been ranked in the top 20 of American public high schools. The school has exceptional facilities, including state of the art computers, a comprehensive library, beautiful athletic fields and a gorgeous campus. Roughly 74 percent of the students average a "B" or better. There are numerous Advanced Placement, independent study, honors and accelerated courses as well as extensive

Great Neck North High School today

resources for students requiring remedial assistance.

Great Neck South High School is located on the former Phipps Estate off Lakeville Road. (Henry Phipps had been a

The Phipps mansion serves as the Administration Building at South High School

Great Neck South High School

17th Century Schoolhouse and Farm still standing in Kings Point are the original farmhouse and old schoolhouse buildings that served the then small, young community - above and below

partner of Andrew Carnegie.) The Phipps mansion serves as the Administration Building. South High School is also a perpetual success story, achieving similar rankings annually. The school is also (predictably) well equipped, as they constantly update their computers and keep the grounds well groomed. Seventy-seven percent of South students earn a "B" average or better.

Both high schools take pride in the fact that an overwhelming majority of their students — 96 percent in North, 99 percent in South — continue on to college, many attending Ivy League universities and some of the best colleges in the world. The schools consistently produce Intel Science Talent Search and Siemens Westinghouse Science and Technology Competition finalists as well as many National Merit finalists, semifinalists, and commended students. College Board scores continually outpace the national average, as do results of standardized testing in the lower grades. Pupils are involved in a wide range of extracurricular subjects and community service endeavors.

The Village School, an alternative program, also serves high school students from all parts of Great Neck. Its registrants follow a non-traditional, more independent, course of study.

In 1812, New York became the first state to mandate a state-wide public school system. Two years later, the Great Neck Common School District Number 7 was established. The Woolley's Brook School was built east of what is now Middle Neck Road across from Old Mill Road.

School was free and met six days a week, 12 months a year. To accommodate students who dropped out for a few months to work the farms during crop season, the academic year was divided into quarters.

Children learned in the Fairview Avenue School from about 1840 to 1869. Then a two-room schoolhouse, complete with belfry and a white picket fence, was erected on Arrandale Avenue. The three primary grades occupied one room while the older children received instruction in a second classroom. Boys and girls had their own entrance. Pupils brought their own slates and sponges. During recess, boys and girls played on opposite sides of a fence in the schoolyard.

Great Neck got its own Board of Education on January 1, 1895 when Union Free School District was formed. That fall, the Board established Great Neck's first high school and qualified for Regents certification with the purchase of a $29 microscope for "Physiology," its first science course. Along with the installation of electricity, a chemistry course was added to the curriculum in 1898; the first science lab was built in 1905. In 1906 Great Neck schools had indoor plumbing installed.

A new three-story school was built on Arrandale in 1900. Price tag: $24,500. Because of increasing enrollment, School No. 2 opened in 1905 on what was later called the Kensington site.

The Adult Program celebrated its 102st anniversary in April of 2003, and has supplied Great Neckers of all ages with quality programming at the Cumberland and Clover Drive centers.

A thick course catalogue includes subjects from the culinary arts to computers. Over 400 courses are offered to more than 6,000 registrants annually.

English as a Second Language is taught at the Clover Drive Adult Learning Center along with GED and EDP diploma programs for those needing high school equivalency degrees. Over 1,200 students who moved to Great Neck from 46 countries attend these classes annually. The Adult Education Program also works with the Great Neck Senior Center with classes such as Water Aerobics and Theater Workshop. Fees for residents are generally nominal.

The North Shore Hebrew Academy, a co-ed modern Orthodox day school, offers a top-notch Jewish and secular education and has expanded as the local Orthodox Jewish community has grown. The school currently has more than 750 students and occupies three campuses, one for preschoolers and elementary school youngsters on Cherry Lane, a middle school on Old Mill Road and a high school in the business park at 175 Community Drive in Lake Success. The school also operates N'Shama, a day camp and young teen travel program in the summertime.

Plans are underway for North Shore Hebrew Academy's new high school cam-

pus, complete with a state-of-the art main building, playing fields and swimming pool. The school will be located off the North Service Road of the Long Island Expressway in Lake Success, at the top of Community Drive.

The Long Island Hebrew Academy, another yeshiva, is located on Cutter Mill Road. Across the street from it is the Chabad Silverstein Hebrew Academy.

There are numerous other programs for education in Great Neck. Preschools and day care centers include A+ For Kids, Beth HaGan at Temple Israel, C.L.A.S.P., Great Neck Community School, Great Neck Pre-School, Lakeville Nursery School, Romper Room Nursery, Temple Beth-El of Great Neck Nursery School and Temple Emanuel Nursery School.

Most temples and churches offer religious instruction through Sunday Schools and after school programs. Other learning opportunities are available through Levels and local chapters of the Boy Scouts and Girl Scouts.

Weekends are a hub of activity at parks and playing fields. Depending on the season, youngsters play soccer, baseball, judo, softball and basketball through the Police Activity League (P.A.L). There are recreational teams for children from kindergarten through the ninth grade.

During the fall, more than 1500 children play soccer in both a coed league and an all girls soccer league for youth through the ninth grade. Coed teams are named after different countries. Kindergarteners through second graders can also join a winter indoor soccer program. The league offers a weeklong summer soccer camp at the end of August. In the spring, there is both coed baseball for children through the 10th grade plus an all girl's soccer league for girls in the fourth through eighth grade. There is also fall baseball and softball. In the winter, children can select instructional and intramural basketball. Judo is offered for grades 2 through 8.

Faces of Great Neck

While Great Neck has become more of a community town, many notable people have come from Great Neck, or at least made a stop in Great Neck on their respective ways to fame.

Among the writers who have lived in Great Neck in the past 40 years are **Margaret Wise Brown**, author of

Herman Wouk

Goodnight Moon, **Herman Wouk**, whose numerous books include *The Winds of War, War and Remembrance* and *Marjorie Morningstar.* Among the 10 books written by Great Neck sociologist **William Helmreich** is *Against All Odds: Holocaust Survivors and the Successful Lives They Built in America.*

Johanna Hurwitz, author of *Aldo Applesauce, The Cold and Hot Winter* and many more prize-winning children's books, was once a children's librarian at the main branch. **Gordan Korman**, author of *Beware the Fish* and *A Semester in the Life of a Garbage Bag,* **Ellen Conford**, author of dozens of books including *A Job for Jenny Archer* and *Starring in Gorilla My Dreams,* and the late **Esphyr Slobodkina**, author and illustrator of *Caps for Sale,* are also among the many local children's writers. The CBS news correspondent **Dan Raviv** grew up in Great Neck. He is the author of *Behind the Uprising* and *Every Spy a Prince.* **David J. Silverman** is the author of *Taxes for Dummies.* **Ira Levin**, author of *Rosemary's Baby* and *The Boys from Brazil* was a one-time Kings Point resident.

Nor is there is a shortage of funny guys. **Alan King** resides in Oscar Hammerstein's former mansion in the Kennilworth community in Kings Point. King, a world-famous comedian, has

Joey Adams

appeared frequently in the movies such as *Sunsine State, Rush Hour 2, Casino* and on Friars Club roasts. Baby boomers recognize him instantly from his 90 appearances on *The Ed Sullivan Show.* King also wrote *Help! I'm a Prisoner in a Chinese Bakery.* The late comedian **Joey Adams,** a syndicated comedy columnist whose prolific career ranged from vaudeville to the Catskills to television, lived on Woodland Place in Saddle Rock Estates. The actor **Paul Newman** once lived on Station Road and the artist **Louise Nevelson** taught sculpture in the

Paul Newman

Adult Education program. The artist **Max Weber** also resided in Great Neck. **Kenneth Cole**, the fashion designer known

Kenneth Cole

for his men's and women's footwear, graduated from Great Neck North in 1972. **Mary Cleave,** the astronaut, was in the Great Neck North class of 1965. She has been on two space shuttle flights.

The tunesmith, **Ervin Drake**, a renowned composer and lyricist, wrote classics like *I Believe,* the raindrop ballad. His *It Was A Very Good Year,* was popularized by Frank Sinatra. He is the vice chairman of the Songwriters Hall of Fame and the vice president of the Songwriters Guild of America.

Known for his collection of bawdy songs and parodies, over the course of his 60-plus year career, the folksinger **Oscar Brand** has released more than

Oscar Brand

Al Grey

90 albums. The late jazz great **Al Grey** lived in Kings Point and frequently performed at Steppingstone Park. The composer and pianist

Morton Gould also lived in Great Neck, first in Russell Gardens and later in Thomaston.

Morton Gould

Marvin Hamlisch, the Oscar winning composer of films, songs

Marvin Hamlisch

and musicals, including the scores for *The Way We Were* and the soundtrack to the movie *Sting* has also lived in Great Neck.

The legendary movie star **Joan Crawford** may have been in the 1949 film Flamingo Road but she lived for a time on Station Road in Great Neck. Joan once said, "I think the most important thing a woman can have, next to talent, of course - is her hairdresser." **Martha Raye**, the singer, actress, comedian and dancer, whose career spanned from Vaudeville to Hollywood, had a nightclub in her Harbor Hills home.

Joan Crawford

Martha Raye

D e b o r a h Schindler, who grew up in Great Neck, recently produced the Jennifer Lopez movie *Made in Manhattan* and the 1998 movie *How Stella Got Her Grove Back*.

Dr. Mathilde Krim, the famous AIDS researcher and scientist and founder/chairwoman of the American Foundation for AIDS Research, has a waterfront country estate on Dock Lane in Kings Point. Part of the celebrity swirl - Elizabeth Taylor is AMFAR's national founding chairwoman - Dr. Krim is frequently a boldface name in Liz Smith's star-studded columns. Her Hollywood connections have helped raise millions for AMFAR. In 2000, Dr. Krim received a Presidential Medal of Freedom from President Clinton, the country's highest civilian honor.

Dr. Krim's late husband, entertainment lawyer **Arthur B. Krim,** was a former chairman of Orion Pictures and United Artists and the producer of more than 1,000 movies, including *High Noon, 10, Arthur, One Flew Over the Cuckoo's Nest, Rocky and Annie Hall*. Krim, who died in 1994, became interested in films through his work as a lawyer. When United Artists, which was founded in 1919 by **Charlie Chaplin, Mary Pickford, Douglas Fairbanks**, and **DW Griffith**, fell on hard times, Krim and his next door neighbor, **Robert Benjamin**, took over the management the motion picture studio in 1951 and turned it around, eventually selling it to Transamerica. Later, Krim headed Orion Pictures from 1978 to 1992. Krim was also an influential advisor to three presidents: John F. Kennedy, Jimmy Carter and Lyndon B. Johnson. During the Johnson Administration, the Krims had a room at the White House.

Andy Kaufman, the late world-famous comedian and sitcom star best known for his role as Latka Gravas in *Taxi*, grew up in Great Neck. Part of the 1999 biographical movie *Man on the Moon*, starring Jim Carrey, was shot around the corner from Kaufman's boyhood home on Robin Way in Saddle Rock Estates.

Andy Kaufman

Before Andy was a year old, he

reached from his crib to put the needle back on a phonograph record and keep it playing. When he was 7, the Kaufmans - also including his dad, Stanley, mother Janice, brother Michael and sister Carol -- moved to Kings Point. Carol Kaufman Kerman recalled Andy listening to music, creating and putting on shows in the den. Sometimes the siblings would perform together in front of an imaginary audience. He did magic tricks and told jokes to family and friends.

"While all the other kids were out playing ball and stuff, I used to stay in my room and imagine that there was a camera in the wall. And I used to really believe that I was putting on a television show and that it was going out to somewhere in the world," Kaufman once said.

When Andy was 8 years old, unbeknownst to his parents, he took out an ad in the Pennysaver offering his services as an entertainer for birthday parties. The phone soon started ringing with requests for engagements. Stanley ended up helping him out with the equipment. At the parties, Andy showed *L'il Rascals* films and clips from *Creature from the Black Lagoon*. Then he would do magic tricks, play the guitar and let the children record themselves on a reel-to-reel recorder, which always elicited lots of giggles.

Andy loved Elvis Presley. Long before a swarm of Elvis impersonators emerged, Kaufman mastered the King of Rock and Roll's moves and swivels. Once he even hitchhiked to Las Vegas to meet the star. By the time Andy got to Great Neck North High School, he could do a masterful Elvis imitation but was a C- student . He graduated 419th out of 461 in the class of 1967. Kaufman was on the high school wrestling team and was a chin up champion.

Kaufman drove a taxi about town, picking up passengers at the station and dropping off customers at Frederick's or Chopmeat Charlie's, where diners plucked their meals off model train cars that chugged around the restaurant. He had a paper route at age 14, but threw the newspapers in a sewer.

Andy often played pranks. Once he snipped the roses from his father's prized rose garden and blamed it on his brother Michael, who was 2 and still in the crib. Michael got a beating. He waited 12 years before he said "it was me." Another time, Andy and Michael painted their parents' brand-new furniture white.

Andy was a smash hit in comedy clubs and appeared on the inaugural show of Saturday Night Live. Michael recalled Andy only working 2 days a week at the hit sitcom *Taxi* because he didn't need to practice his lines. He knew all his lines which made some of the other actors envious. Andy would rather create new stuff someplace else or meditate while the other actors were running lines.

But throughout his career Andy insisted he was not a comedian. He didn't want the people to think they had to laugh. "I never told a joke in my life," he once said.

Andy Kaufman died in 1984 at age 35 of a rare form of lung cancer.

Voices of Great Neck: Alan King

Alan King

The comedian, movie star and author Alan King has lived in Great Neck for 41 years and gets much of his material from his life on the peninsula. King raised three children in the Oscar Hammerstein mansion in Kings Point. His six grandchildren often come to visit. Some reflections on what's kept him here:

"Great Neck was always 'hot.' It was an upscale community. I came from a $26,000 ranch house in Rockville Centre. This was, to say the least, living in the Hammerstein mansion, high on the hog.

The reason I've stayed here is I love the community. My country club, Fresh Meadows, is 10 minutes away."

"My favorite restaurant was here and it was Navona and now it's Stresa, in Manhasset, just a hop and a skip. I love the Kensington Deli. I get my corned beef once a week. Then the fish place my grandchildren like a lot is Turquoise, by the station. I don't have to go very far to get good food."

"I have been very comfortable. My office is in New York and I am an hour away. Everyone wants to know where my summer home is. It's right next door to my winter home. I built a studio and a guest home."

"I'm a big rose nut. I grow all kinds of flowers. I have had the same gardener, Santelli's for 40 years, doing my gardens. I love looking out at the water. A mountain never changes. The water always changes."

Voice of Great Neck: Ervin Drake

Ervin Drake

The legendary songwriter Ervin Drake moved to Great Neck in 1951 with his first wife, Ada, and his one year old baby, Linda. Five years later his other daughter, Betsy, was born.

"It was a lot less congested," Drake recalled. "For me for many, many years it was a bedroom community. The only thing I did here besides go to the Lake Success golf course was sleep here. I really had a good time. I'd go on the course after being in the city with the ravages of television and Tin Pan Alley and I'd come home with a smile on my face."

In 1975, after Ada died, Drake met Edith Berman, owner of Bermaine, a flourishing cosmetics and wig business for women that was located next to the Squire Theatre for some 35 years. They married.

Edith was involved in the community and Drake started going to parties with her.

Like many Great Neckers, the Drakes gave their home a massive do-over. "Just this past year, I parted with half a million bucks to have a second floor put on my house," Drake said. "It was a ranch." They added a second floor with a gymnasium, a master bath that could double as a skating rink, a huge master bedroom and a dumb waiter. Why didn't they just move?

"I am within walking distance of the railroad," Drake said. "The train line is the best line on Long Island, between 25 and 30 minutes. That convenience is marvelous."

Even though he owned apartments in Manhattan until 1998, Drake always came home to Great Neck.

"We leave the city, whether we drive or take the train and immediately it's different," he said. "The air is different. It's fresher. It's cooler. We can walk directly onto grass, you are walking on sod instead of on concrete. Where you enter is your own home. You are not rocketing up vertically to the 32nd floor of some skyscraper where you have your own cliff home. To us that makes a big difference."

More Boldface Names

David Baltimore

The success of Great Neckers is legendary in many arenas. Among the other well-known names who have resided in Great Neck over the past forty years are:

David Baltimore, the Nobel Prize winner, grew up in Great Neck and graduated from the public school system in 1956. Only 14 years later he earned the top science accolade for his contributions to AIDS research.

Alfred Levitt, the builder of 12,000 cookie cutter ranches and 6,000 Cape Cod homes in Levittown, raised his own family in a 15-room ranch on Kings Point Road in Kings Point. He

Alfred Levitt

also built substantial brick colonials and Tudor homes in Great Neck, including Saddle Rock Estates.

Bruce Paltrow

The actress Gwyneth Paltrow's late father, **Bruce Paltrow**, became a bar mitzvah at Temple Beth El. A member of the class of 1956, director **Francis Ford Coppola** graduated from Great Neck North, though he only lived in Great Neck for a short time. Coppola made the hit movie *Apocalypse Now*, as well as the *Godfather* trilogy. His sister, **Talia Shire**, also graduated from the Great Neck Public School District, earning her diploma at South in 1964. She went on to play Adrian, the

Francis Ford Coppola, Great Neck High School Photo, 1956

Talia Shire

wife of Sylvester Stallone, in the *Rocky* movies, and played the role of Connie in her older brother's *Godfather* flicks.

Dawn Steel graduated in Talia's class. Steel went on to become the head of Paramount and Columbia Pictures. She produced the hit movies *Top Gun, Fatal Attraction,* and *When Harry Met Sally.*

Julia Phillips grew up in Great Neck and won a best picture Oscar for co-producing *The Sting.*

Dawn Steel

Great Neck's "golden girl" Sarah Hughes' parade was the biggest ever held in Great Neck. Left: Sarah maintained her cheery smile, enthusiastically waving her gold medal. Left bottom and top right: Thousands marched along and gathered at the end of the parade in front of Great Neck North High School. Top right Jewels by Viggi, Danny and Viggi Arbusman present Sarah with a gold Cartier watch to match her gold medal.

The most recent Great Neck star is **Sarah Hughes**, who was awarded the Gold Medal for her figure skating performance in the 2002 Salt Lake City Winter Olympics when she was 16. One of six children, Hughes lived at home while she did triple axels and skated her way to the sport's grandest prize. Hughes has earned a number of other awards, as well, including the much-coveted Espy sports award. A parade in her honor on Middle Neck Road after her Olympic championship attracted 40,000 people and numerous politicians. Hughes is an honors student in the Great Neck North High School's Class of 2003, plays the violin in the school orchestra and earned early admittance to Harvard. In the wake of her victory, she met President George W. Bush, was pictured on a Wheaties cereal box and featured in numerous national publications. Sarah was also written into the lyrics in a version of Adam Sandler's *Hanukkah Song*. The hometown hero spread good cheer visiting patients at Schneider Children's Hospital as part of a program called *Heroes for Health* and was the subject of an NBC special, *Sarah Hughes: A Life in Balance*.

Sarah was a runner-up to Michelle Kwan at the 2001 U.S. National Championships and finished third at the 2001 World Championships. She was the 1998 Junior National Champion and was the Bronze medalist at the 2002 U.S. Figure Skating Championships, qualifying her for the Olympic Team.

Home of Dame Nellie Melba

Summer home of the famous Australian opera singer who was the first Australian to debut at Covent Garden in London at the turn of the century. Chefs honored her by naming creations like "Peach Melba" and "Melba Toast" for her.

Residence of Walter P. Chrysler

Built in 1900, built by Henri Bendel, later sold to the Chrysler family and then ultimately sold to the United States government in 1938 to serve as the home of the U.S. Merchant Marine Academy. Now known as Wiley Hall.

Residence of Alan King

Previously home to the late, great Oscar Hammerstein III, part of the famed musical team of Rodgers and Hammerstein, this glorious Tudor mansion has an unparalleled view of the Long Island Sound and, for more than forty years, has been the home of actor, comedian Alan King.

Home of Joey Adams

"My doctor has a great stress test. It's called 'the bill.'"
This 1939 Normandy Tudor was once home to the Borscht Belt comedian. Later, the author of this book lived in this Saddle Rock Estates home.

Home of Andy Kaufman

Early in his act , Andy once ate a bowl of potatoes onstage, went to sleep for 20 minutes in a sleeping bag. Then got up and took a bow.

Residence of Joan Crawford

Once at a MGM party, F. Scott Fitzgerald was introduced to Joan Crawford, he mentioned to her that he was working on a screenplay in which she was to star. Her reply was, "Write well Mr. Fitzgerald! Write well!" To an associate, Scott quipped, "Bitch." (He showed restraint.)

Residence of F. Scott Fitzgerald

F. Scott and Zelda moved to Great Neck when he was 25, to be closer to Broadway. It was here that Scott observed the life that he would incorporate into his novel, The Great Gatsby (Great Neck is the model for West Egg).

Home of W.C. Fields

"I always keep a supply of stimulant handy in case I see a snake-- which I also keep handy." This Mediterranean style house , reminiscent of the Beverly Hills mansions of the time. The master bathroom boasts initials on the tiles , "W.C."

Frank Lloyd Wright House

Wright's architectural philosophy, built in 1937 for Ben Rebhuhn. This house is similar to the Vosburgh house in Michigan, except this house is in the Usonian style, and the Vosburgh residence (built 21 years before) is in the Prairie style.

Residence of Paulette Goddard

Born Pauline Marion Levy in Great Neck. She was "Peaches", the Ziegfeld Girl at 14, then a Goldwyn Girl, and Hal Roach comic. She met Charlie Chaplin on a yacht and married him secretly at sea. He wrote "Modern Times" and "The Great Dictator" for her.

Home of Groucho Marx

Film Star and a master at delivering one-liners, lived in Thomaston for 8 Years.. - "A man is as young as the woman he feels, Now there's a man with an open mind - you can feel the breeze from here! "

Residence of George M. Cohan

Majestically standing on a bluff overlooking the Long Island Sound, this house was the home of this legendary American musical icon. Later on, it was home to Walter Annenburg, American philanthropist and Ambassador. Recently, it was added to the list of national landmarked homes and is currently being restored.

Voices of Great Neck:
Johanna Hurwitz, children's author

Johanna Hurwitz

My family moved from Manhattan, where I was born, to Great Neck in the fall of 1974. Twenty-eight years later I am amazed that I have spent almost half my life in this community. We could not have found a better place to live.

My children attended Kensington-Johnson School and then South Middle and Senior High School. They had excellent teachers and made many lasting friendships. I loved the fact that they could walk to elementary school, and from our Great Neck Estates home they could also walk easily into town. They had the independence of going for pizza, or to Woolworths, or the movies, on their own. It was just like my own childhood in the Bronx, but not the way we had lived in Manhattan. There I had to supervise their every move because of concern for their safety.

For the first year after our move, I commuted regularly to Manhattan where I worked as a school librarian. The contrast between the city and my new home was always a surprise to me. I would get off the train with the other commuters (mostly men in those days) and walk home marveling at the wisteria that grew on Elm Street (I'd never seen wisteria before!) and how so many people would nod in friendly greeting, even when they didn't actually know me. Subsequently, when I began working in the children's department at the Great Neck Library the numbers of people who recognized me grew and grew. My children claimed it was impossible for us to have a slice of pizza at Gino's without being interrupted by half a dozen youngsters or their mothers asking for a recommendation for their next book report. "This is small town life," I told them.

Although I had been writing for years, it was within months of our move, that my first book was accepted for publication. So my career as a children's book writer has always been associated in my mind with Great Neck. And from Great Neck, I have found many inspirations and topics to write about: the closing of K-J School was the subject of my book *School Spirit,* the tragic death of the Ed Armheim of Levels inspired *Even Stephen,* our move to the suburbs was the subject of *Aldo Applesauce,* and when the late Ellen Hirschland's grandchildren came to spend the summer in Great Neck, I got the idea for my book *The Hot & Cold Summer.*

Now my children have grown and are out in the world and leading their own lives with children of their own. But my husband and I remain in Great Neck. Some of our neighbors and friends have moved away and others have passed away. But the tall trees in my yard and the friendliness of the people on the street remains. I love living here even when the traffic on Middle Neck Road gives me cause for shudder. The street fairs, the shops, the good friends are all very special to me. When I travel around the country and visit schools in other cities and states, children ask me where I live. "Great Neck," I say. "It's just across the street from another community called Little Neck." They always laugh at the name and think I've said something funny. But of course, you and I know it's not a joke, it's the truth."

Voice of Great Neck:
Edna Zelan

Great Neck has changed oh-so-much! I remember the small High School that was on Arrandale Ave. I was in the 8th grade with a teacher who traveled all around the world and I was so intrigued about her that this was what I wanted to do with my life. I believe it was in May, 1920, one morning I woke up and the whole string of classrooms were burning down to the ground. I was so heart broken."

"About 1922, I remember The Playhouse was a small little theater. I was 15 years old and I had walked there - in those days nobody was afraid of anything. Thomas Meighan was *the* actor at that time. The day it opened up they had a book with his picture. It was all so lovely. When they finished a reel they would have to turn on the lights and put the next reel on to continue the movie. I'm sitting in the theater watching the movie and there's Thomas Meighan sitting next to me in the theater watching his own picture - I just gasped."

"A lot of the theater people lived in Grenwolde Park in Kings Point. Not only the actors but all the people who made the pictures."

"The main roads were two lanes all along and being the oldest in the family, it was my duty to go with my father to dump the garbage. There were no garbage collectors in those days and we would fertilize the forest with our garbage. Everybody did that - it was fertilizer!"

"Our toilet was in the yard and was made into a house. It was my job to keep it going. We had a potbelly stove to warm three bedrooms. The house is next to the Village School on Middle Neck Road and it's still there."

"I remember going to the big store in the 1950's called 'Wanamakers.' They were gorgeous. I remember the great stairs going up. They expanded that tremendously now. Great Neck Gardens -- it has changed so!"

"It's interesting when you're here and you're living through the times that are changing. You sort of roll with the changes and go right on as though it's the way it should be, or has been, or is going to be -- and you don't realize that this passage of time means so much -- when there are so many changes. You just kind of roll with the punches -- and survive."

Edna will be 96 this year and still lives in Great Neck.

Making a Difference

From a time when 17th century settlers searched for religious independence to when half of a community pulled the other half out of the Great Depression to today's UCF tennis tournaments and successful blood drives, Great Neck has been a place where movers and shakers and people who make a difference come to live. Here's a look at a few of those people.

Joseph Gurwin's main hobby is philanthropy. A retired industrialist from Great Neck, his philanthropic endeavors include the Rosalind and Joseph Gurwin Jewish Geriatric Center in Commack, a top-of-the-line nursing facility and the first kosher nursing home to open in Suffolk County. A few years ago he also financed the development of the Gurwin II TechSat, 106-pound microsatellite packed with scientific experiments that orbits the earth with his name on it, measuring ozone and radiation. It also transmits images of the earth's surface. A project of the Technion-Israel Institute of Technology, it can be used by amateur radio operators to communicate with each other. "If you can do something to make the world better so future generations can improve on it, that's what it's all about," Mr. Gurwin once told *The New York Times.*

Mr. Gurwin, whose parents died in the Holocaust, preferred playing soccer to studying, and only came to the United States in 1936 at age 16 because he had failed two subjects in school — Lithuanian and Latin. He later dropped out of night school at City College, but built a fortune manufacturing military products like bulletproof vests and parachute drop equipment for the government.

To help at-risk youth, Great Neck philanthropists Lilo and Gerard Leeds founded the Institute for Student Achievement. The organization works with middle and high schoolers on Long Island and beyond to improve quality of life for children who might not otherwise complete school

In 1971, Mr. Leeds started the high-technology media company CMP Media Inc. with the trade publication *The Electronic Buyer's News,* working out of his living room in Great Neck. The next year, the first issue of *The Electronic Engineering Times* was printed. Years later they took the company public.

In 1990, the couple donated $21 million from the stock sale to found The Institute for Student Achievement, then known as the Institute for Community Development. Education, the Leedses contend, is critical to breaking the cycle of poverty.

One of the institute's programs, STAR, which stands for Success Through Academic Readiness, features four years of daily academic enrichment, counseling and support. The Comet middle-school program for 12- to 14-year-olds, began in 1993 as Children of Many Educational Talents. Its goal is to help youngsters improve attitudes and academic performance. With the help of the Institute, grades, attendance and poor attitudes improve and the vast majority of students go on to college.

Additionally, CMP was the first company on Long Island to offer day care. The Leedses later sold the company, also support other child care organizations, arts organizations, and other charities. "What we're doing now with the institute," Mr. Leeds told *The New York Times,* is more exciting than building a company. Our goal is to someday be at a point where a million children are in programs like this, and someday further than that, all children will get the education they need to succeed."

The name Tilles is recognizable not just in Great Neck but all over Long Island. That's not only because of the premier family development business but because of their philanthropic efforts. The Tilles' of Great Neck have brought performances by the New York Philharmonic and the Metropolitan Opera Orchestra to local audiences. Roger Tilles and his brother Peter Tilles were major benefactors of The Tilles Center, a performing arts hall on the Long Island University Campus of C.W. Post in Old Brookville. Roger Tilles is the chair of the center. "We believe the performing arts are not some ornaments that are casual accessories to our lives. They contribute to the very essence of who we are as individuals and to the quality of life we seek to create as a region," Roger Tilles said. He is also a past president of Temple Beth El and a founding member and chairman of the Association for a Better Long Island, a pro-business organization representing $20 billion in commercial, industrial and retail space throughout the region.

The Face of Great Neck: Henry Viscardi, Jr.

Henry Vicardi, Jr.

Henry Viscardi, Jr. has lived his life accentuating the positive. His lifelong mission has been to help the disabled realize their abilities and capitalize on them. Viscardi, a long-time Great Neck legend, founded the internationally recognized National Center for Disability Services, a multi-faceted, state-of-the art-educational training and research institution in Albertson.

Born without legs, he spent the first six years of his life as a charity patient in a hospital ward for crippled children. He has served as an adviser to presidents, penned eight books and received over 20 honorary doctorates. The center is a product of Abilities Inc., a venture Dr. Viscardi started over 49 years ago out of a West Hempstead garage with eight handicapped adults — legless, armless, blind and paralyzed — who were considered unemployable by traditional standards. Ten years later, Abilities, a competitive not-for-profit enterprise, had 475 employees building electronic components.

In 1962, he founded the Human Resources School (which was later renamed in his honor) to educate severely disabled children who otherwise would have to study at home or in a hospital bed. The Henry Viscardi School - a tuition free institution chartered by New York State, has 220 pupils in pre-kindergarten through high school, 40 percent of whom come from New York City. New technologies, long-distance learning capabilities and a website are allowing the trend setting work there to be shared with the disabled all over the globe. The Kings Pointer has resided in Great Neck for 56 of his 91-plus years. He retired as chief executive officer in 1981. Educating and training thousands of people with disabilities, and inspiring them to lead active, fulfilling lives, Dr. Viscardi's work continues to have an impact on the lives of Long Islanders and their families. In 1997, almost 300 people with disabilities were placed into employment on Long Island and an additional 327 found employment elsewhere with the center's help.

The 9-11 Memorials

They were not famous. But among the nearly 3000 people who lost their lives in the World Trade Center tragedy on Sept. 11, 2001 were six Great Neckers: Jonathan Ielpi, the assistant chief of the Vigilant Fire

Company in Great Neck and a member of the New York City Fire Department, Squad 288 perished when he responded to the calls. Others lost include Andrew Stergiopoulos, Christopher Frank, Frederick Kuo Jr., Richard Yun Choon (Lee) and Josh Vitale.

The Twin Towers were visible from the Saddle Rock Bridge. Following the attack, residents gathered on the bridge, from which there is a view of the Manhattan skyline, watching the smoke billow in the distance. Residents, family members, friends and passersby held prayer vigils, brought flowers, and wrote messages of hope and remembrance along the walls of the span. Later, a flagpole was erected and the bridge was renamed the 9-11 Memorial Bridge.

In November 2002, a memorial plaque was unveiled. A pocket park and sitting area at Grace Avenue and Middle Neck Road, dedicated by the Great Neck Chamber of Commerce and the Village of Great Neck Plaza, to the six community members lost in the attacks.

In a spontaneous tribute, messages of hope and remembrance were scrawled on the walls and railings of the Saddle Rock Bridge. Candles flickered, prayers were said and flowers were left on the span, along with a poignant personal memento: Jonathan Ielpi's beloved hockey jersey. The bridge was later rededicated as the 9-11 Memorial Bridge.

ARTS ENTERTAI
ARTS ENTERT

MENT & MEDIA

NMENT & MEDIA

"I love Great Neck" says Ken James. " Because it is green & safe, like an oasis. It's a unique place to live! - near the highways and the people are fabulous."

As a kid, Ken grew up in Brooklyn, idolizing entertainment people & performers like Neil Diamond, The Tokens, Murray the Kay and more. As the son of a musician, one would have thought it was natural for Ken to end up in the music business. Against his fathers wishes, & hopes for a better future, Ken could not ignore his calling, to entertain.

After graduating, he proceeded to perform at various resorts in the Catskill Mountains. Fast forward to 1977, Ken & his family moved to Great Neck and set up shop at 216 Lakeville Rd. In the 20 years plus since that time, Ken James Productions, has become one of the area's

premier entertainment & production companies, where dreams come true..

Creating elaborate & different parties, designed for his wonderful clients is an ongoing endeavor. "We even had an Organ Grinder & Monkey the client wanted, - that to a 20 piece big band. We worked with many stars like BB King, The Shirelles, Jays and the Americans and even did Murray the "K"s wedding. I remember the Tito Puente' event drew over 400 guests at a gold coast country club."

Ken James Productions prides itself in their ability to customize each party, so no two events are ever alike. Building strong relationships with many professional performers, guarantees clients the highest quality entertainment. *Check them out...*

KEN JAMES PRODUCTIONS LTD   216 LAKEVILLE RD, GREAT NECK 11020   PHONE: 800.564.0372   WWW.KENJAMESPRODUCTIONS.COM

Successfully Serving the Nation for Over 35 Years.

Your Wedding...
Make Its Moments
Last Forever.

Dwight Howard Entertainment

Making Musical
Memories That
Last A Lifetime.

516.829.0040

www.dwighthowardmusic.com

ARTS, ENTERTAINMENT AND MEDIA

The Great Neck Arts Center is a prime example of a community's dedication to and appreciation for arts and culture.

The comprehensive arts school, gallery and performance center near the Squire Theatre on Middle Neck Road enriches local cultural life with a wide-ranging program, including a salon series of concerts held in private homes on the peninsula and out-

reach programs with local assisted living facilities, art receptions, natural juried art shows and film series.

Classes, offered Monday to Saturday, range from chess, drama, ballet, cartooning to music instruction. Paintings, prints, photography and sculpture by prominent artists are featured in the art gallery. The center also offers classical, jazz and popular concerts, panel discussions and theatre parties.

Regina Gil, a local artist, teacher and founder of the Artists Network of Great Neck, led the effort to make the non profit center a hallmark of the peninsula.

The Great Neck Arts Center opened in 1995 in the basement of St. Paul's Episcopal Church off Grace

Avenue. It moved to its present location two years later and continues to expand its offerings. Since 1996 it has been an affiliate of the John F. Kennedy Center for the Performing Arts in Washington, D.C., in partnership with the Plainview/Old Bethpage Schools.

The Great Neck House, run by the Park District, is a thriving cultural center offering concerts, art classes, exhibits, movie nights and fireside recitals in the Tudor-style mansion on Arrandale Avenue. A current park card is required to register and attend these events.

A full roster of classes is offered year-round, including acting, aerobics, ceramics, cooking, crafts, dance, drama, exercise and nature workshops, plus a rainy day animated film series. Card and games tables are available, along with meeting rooms for local organizations that apply to use them. And the Great Neck House is a prime venue for local artists, sculptors and photographers to show their work.

On the first Sunday in June at 1 p.m., New Residents' Day introduces newcomers to all park district amenities. Park cards, parking stickers, tennis stickers and permits are also obtainable at the Great Neck House. Non-park district residents may register for classes at an extra fee depending on available space.

Aspiring musicians at all levels can also take classes at the Great Neck Music Center on Middle Neck Road in the Village of Great Neck. Classes start

with Kindermusik and Suzuki for young children. Music lovers can participate in chorus and instrumental ensembles, music theory, ear training and music appreciation classes. There is also an advanced pre-conservatory program.

The Squire movie theatre is usually packed on Fridays, Saturdays and Sundays, with lines for first-run films sometimes stretching up the block, and, for popcorn, three deep at the counter. Great Neck's only movie house opened in the 1930's on Middle Neck Road across the street from Lesser's Playhouse in a converted garage. The Squire, like most cinemas at the times, only showed films on its single screen for two to three day intervals. Classics that appeared in the early days of the Squire include *Love Before Breakfast* with Carol Lombard, *Destry Rides Again* with Marlene Dietrich and James Stewart, *In the Navy* with Abbott and Costello and *King Kong*.

In the 1980s, the Squire became a triplex and after it was acquired by the Clearview Cinema Group in 1998, Great Neck's only movie house became a multiplex with 8 silver screens. One of its theatres was named after Francis Ford Coppola, a graduate of Great Neck North high school and the same graduating class as former Village of Great Neck Plaza Major Robert Rosegarten.

Voices of Great Neck: Regina Gil

Founder of the Great Neck Arts Center:

Regina Gil

Moving to Great Neck in 1976 was a big step for my family and me. I had grown up in New York City, attended the High School of Music & Art, City College, and School of Visual Arts, among others. The Museum of Modern Art, The Met (both the museum and the opera), Greenwich Village, the 42nd Street Library, the galleries and the street shows -- all were a significant part of

128

my education. The art and culture of New York City will always occupy a special place in my heart and memory. Therefore, when my husband Joe and I considered moving to the suburbs, it was most important that we find a community with a commitment to the arts, education and cultural endeavors, not only for ourselves, but also for our children.

Great Neck had a long history of artistic excellence. It had been the home to a galaxy of stars of stage, screen, literature, painting and sculpture for generations. It already had a local arts center where I could get involved and send my children for classes. Add that to the beauty of the peninsula, the great schools, libraries and civic organizations and it felt right. Great Neck was our perfect choice.

But times change. The arts began to take a back seat to other curricular imperatives. Audiences began to diminish for concerts of classical music; book stores closed; art galleries offered posters instead of cutting edge exhibits; movies became

more violent, less thought-provoking; and a dance performance attracted only loyal fans of dance or family and friends of the performers. Great Neck was no exception. To my dismay, in the early 80's, the arts center that had attracted my family to this town closed its doors and the building was sold.

The cultural heart of Great Neck, the Arts, couldn't just die or fade away. I could not sit idly by and let the arts silently slip into oblivion. I had to take action for my children, my neighbor's children and future generations. An arts center is a living thing.

It draws life from the artists, performers, intellects, teachers, students and visitors. It grows when voices and ideas are exchanged freely. When founding the Great Neck Arts Center, I was able to draw on my resources as an artist, teacher, parent, citizen and community activist. The project grew because the idea of a viable and dynamic visual and performing arts center in Great Neck, once again, attracted all the good people committed to the arts. And there were so many resources here in Great Neck.

I am still in awe of the spectacular residents of this community who joined my first tentative steps and helped restore the arts to a position of prominence. Those residents reflect a cross-section of a healthy community. Politicians, civic leaders, artists, singers, actors, full-time moms, doctors, lawyers, architects, teachers, school administrators, librarians, business people, store and restaurant owners, Kiwanians, Rotarians and Lions Club members --- everyone recognized how important it would be to the community to bring the arts back.

And the Arts (with a capital "A") are back! This community turns out for multiple concerts on a Sunday afternoon, for new exhibits at galleries, for dance and music and art and good films. Young families are moving in and seeking out classes for their children, much the way my generation did years ago. These new residents experience the joy when their children act, sing, play instruments, paint and sculpt, fence and tell jokes. They are aware that exposure to a real artistic experience will enrich them in a profound way and they take classes they never had time for before. Or maybe they're just reorganizing their time to make room for the arts. We still have a way to go before Nassau County can be compared with New York City from a cultural vantage point, but here in Great Neck, the arts are alive and growing and I am glad my husband and I made our decision to live here.

Voices of Great Neck: Gordon Korman

Gordon Korman

Korman, the author of dozens of books for young readers, moved to Great Neck four years ago. "We moved to Great Neck from Manhattan when our first child was born, so for us it was the classic city-suburbs switch. We traded Greenwich Village for a back yard, nice parks, and superior schools. I think that's why it took a while for us to realize just what a special community we were now a part of.

It still blows my mind that, despite its size, diversity, and cosmopolitan feel, Great Neck is, in the end, a small town. My wife teaches in the Great Neck schools, and when we walk down Middle Neck Road, I feel like I'm glad-handing with the mayor. She knows everybody; she's kissing babies; holding court in line at the bagel store. There are no degrees of separation around here.

We're locals now. We've nailed down all the shortcuts to the expressway; we can find parking in Great Neck Plaza; we know the good trick-or-treating streets for Halloween. Like so many before us, we came for the family life, and stayed for much, much more."

"Mr. Great Neck" Remembers Great Neck

David Lurie

David Lurie, owner of Lurie Realty, past president of the former Great Neck Real Estate Board, the Great Neck Chamber of Commerce and a former trustee of the Village of Great Neck and chairperson of the Great Neck Crafts Fair, discussed his memories of the peninsula in the 1940's and 1950's in an interview in the *Great Neck News*.

"I remember watching my friend falling off her horse at the corner of Middle Neck and Maple, nobody got hurt. I remember the blacksmith checking the horse located at the location of Kolson Hardware. I remember setting up bowling pins at the alley under the Masonic Hall Building on Middle Neck and Maple. I remember the Fire Department block party held between Bond Street and Middle Neck on Grace. There was a vacant lot on the corner of Middle Neck and that's where the games of chance were set up. There was only one house on the street and, of course, the Colony House Hotel. I remember angle parking on Middle Neck Road and storekeepers would carry your packages out to your car, if you honked and waved at them. In those days everyone knew everyone's name and were greeted accordingly. I remember trips with my father on dirt roads up in the wilds of Kings Point and getting "lost" between the estates and farms. I remember parking one night with my date in front of an old Colonial home when we were suddenly interrupted by a police officer. He told us we could not park in front of the Kings Point Police Headquarters. I remember playing in a grand mansion on Beverly Road at the entrance of Kensington. It had ballrooms, huge chandeliers, loads of bedrooms and huge old fashioned baths. In the garage stood an old dusty Rolls Royce. I was chased out of there regularly by the Kensington police. The site is now a co-op apartment building. The only kosher deli in town was Ben's. Not related to the ones around now. Ben had a relative working in the bakery across the street who would let you know if the cakes and cookies were fresh or not. A slight shake of the head was the signal if the goods were stale or not. These are just some of my memories of the 40's & 50's."

The Media

Great Neck is chronicled in two weekly newspapers, the *Great Neck Record* and the *Great Neck News*. Stories in the Long Island section of *The New York Times* and *Newsday* frequently accent Great Neck. The peninsula also has its own television station, cable television channel 20. In 1991, the nine Great Neck villages and six north shore villages established the Public Access Television Corporation, a not-for-profit service organization. Shirley Bruno served as Access Coordinator from inception to 1991, when she became the Executive Director. Residents of these villages can take studio workshops to learn audiovisual skills and create their own non-commercial programs. Among the Channel 20 highlights are a weekly Friday night service broadcast from Temple Beth El, *French for Travelers* -- a course for those who have a basic level of French -- and *New Playwrights* -- highlighting the winners of PATC's annual play-writing contest and produced in association with the North Shore Community Arts Council. Other shows include *The Grace Grella Show*, hosted by Grace Grella, an intuitive consultant who gives psychic readings to viewers. Iranian entertainment and news in Farsi is broadcast by Yafa Soleimani on a weekly basis on *Ma Va Shoma TV*. In conjunction with Grandparent Advocates Supporting Autistic Kids, Nat Silver features Pat Silver interviewing experts and family members who are involved with autistic children on topics pertaining to autism. Professor Vito DeSimone takes a look at current Italian-American poets, novelists and playwrights on *Italian-American Writers*. Bonnie D. Graham produces the talk shows *Something to Talk About* and *Senior Moments*, inviting locally well-known guests. *Chamber Biz*, a show which premiered in January 2003, hosted by Chamber of Commerce president Elliot S. Rosenblatt, presents activities and businesses of the Great Neck Chamber of Commerce. *ChamberVision* with Chamber of Commerce president Elliot S. Rosenblatt and Bonnie D. Graham was on the air for five years and highlighted local businesses.

LONGISLANDMAPS.COM
THE BEST COMPREHENSIVE INFORMATIONAL ARTISTIC ROAD MAPS AVAILABLE !

E-Z GUIDE TO LONG ISLAND GOLF

An Ideal Addition to Your Golf Event or Tournament Gift Bags!

21" x 36" Fold-Up Road Map to L.I.'s 129 Public & Private Golf Courses. Also includes Listings, Pros, Historical Info, Tips, Phone Numbers, Par of Course & More

AlSO AVAILABLE:

LONG ISLAND GOLF LITHOGRAPHS

24" x 36" Limited Edition Prints. Numbered & Signed. Printed on Premium Heavy Stock Suitable For Framing. (a great value)

E-Z GUIDE TO LONG ISLAND CULTURAL ARTS, ENTERTAINMENT & DINING

21" x 36" Fold-Up Road Map to Museums, Visual & Performing Arts, Art Councils And Near By Dining!

E-Z GUIDE TO LONG ISLAND SCENIC TOWNS, VILLAGES & BACK-ROAD PLACES

21" x 36" Fold-Up Road Map to L.I's Historical Sites, Special Towns & Villages to Visit, Wineries, Farm Stands & Markets, Bed & Breakfasts, Boutiques & Many Other Special Highlights

E-Z GUIDE TO LONG ISLAND ANTIQUES

21" x 36" Fold-Up Road Map to Over 200 Shops, Centers & Auction Houses. Complete Detailed Listing on back Describing Each Place to Find Treasures Right Here on Long Island

For more call:

(631) 226-5234

or visit our web site at

OTHER MAPS ALSO AVAILABLE!
or
Reserve Your Space on the Next Up and Coming Maps
CALL TODAY!

T A R G E T   M A R K E T I N G   &   D E S I G N ,   I N C .

Frank Richard Gencorelli, has been in the practice of architecture since 1980.

His portfolio includes numerous commercial, residential and corporate interiors, as well as restoration projects.

He is an assistant professor at The City University of N. Y.

Member of the National Council of Architectural Registration Boards.

Mr. Gencorelli is currently the Chairman of the Historic Preservation Commission of the Village of Great Neck Plaza, which is in the process of designating historic districts and structures of particular value to the village.

FRANK RICHARD GENCORCELLI, A.I.A., ARCHITECT   8 BOND STREET , GREAT NECK 11021   PHONE: 516.487.4465

Wild Ginger Restaurant

RESTAURANTS & FOOD

Cafe Rustica
Fine Nouvelle Italian Cuisine

Fresh Whole and Filet Fish

For Reservations Please Call
516.829.6464
200 Middle Neck Rd., Great Neck

VESPA
CIBOBUONO

RISTORANTE ITALIANO
516.829.0005
96 NORTHERN BLVD. GREAT NECK

RESTAURANTS

Bruzells
See ad page 140
451 Middle Neck Road, Great Neck, NY 11023
516-482-6600
American Continental and Catering
All Major Credit Cards Excepted
Lunch / 12-3, Tues, Wed, Thurs., Fri. Dinner / 7 days
Reservations Recommended

Bistro Grill (k) Glatt French
Steak House, Sushi - Bar
132 Middle Neck Road, Great Neck, NY 11021
516-829-4428
All Major Credit Cards Excepted
Lunch & Dinner / Sun.-Thurs. 12-11pm Open Saturday
1 Hr. After Sundown-1am, Closed Friday
Reservations Required

Bocca di Rosa
24 Middle Neck Road, Great Neck, NY 11021
516-487-9169
Northern Italian
Amex, MasterCard, Visa
Lunch / Mon.-Fri.12-3 pm
Dinner / Mon.-Fri. 5-10 pm, Sat 4-11pm, Sun. 4-9 pm
Reservations Recommended

138

Bruce's Restaurant & Bakery

See our ad on page 139
34 Middle Neck Road, Great Neck, NY 11021
516-829-CAKE(2253)
Casual Continental
Amex Only
Sun.- Fri. 7am-10pm,
Sat. 7am-11pm

Caffe Classico

See our ad on page 141
76 Middle Neck Road, Great Neck, NY 11021
516-829-8008
Italian Cuisine
Amex, MasterCard, Visa
Open 7 days / Sun.-Fri., 11am-12am,
Sat., 11am-2am
Reservations Recommended on Saturday Nights &
Large Parties

Cafe Rustica

See our ad on page 138
200 Middle Neck Road, Great Neck, NY 11021
516-829-6464
Italian - Filet & Whole Fish
Amex, Discover, MasterCard, Visa
Lunch / Mon.-Fri., 12-3pm,
Dinner / Mon.-Thurs 4:30pm-9:30pm,
Fri. & Sat. 4:30pm -11pm, Sun. 4:30pm-9:30pm
Reservations Needed on Weekends

Camellias Chinese Restaurant

See our ad on page 143
8 Bond Street, Great Neck, NY 11021
516-829-8883
Chinese, Szechuan Cuisine
Amex, Diners, MasterCard, Visa
Open Mon.-Thurs., 11am-10pm, Fri. & Sat., 11am-11pm
Sun. 12noon-9:30pm

Fredricks

See our ad on page 142
14 Grace Avenue, Great Neck, NY 11021
516-487-5437
Mon.-Fri. 6:30am-10:30pm, Sat., 6:30am-12pm,
Sun. 8am-10:30pm

La Gioconda

21 North Station Plaza, Great Neck, NY 11021
516-466-2004
Southern Italian
Amex, Diners, MasterCard, Visa
Lunch / Tues.-Fri. 12-3 pm , Sat 1-3 pm
Dinner / Tues. Thurs. 3-10 pm, Fri 3-11pm, Sat. 3-11pm,
Sun 1-10 pm Dinner, Closed Monday
Reservations Recommended

La Rotonda Pizza Restaurant

See our ad on page 143
8 Bond Street, Great Neck, NY 11021
516-466-9596
Southern Italian
MasterCard, Visa / Mon.-Thurs. 12noon-9:30pm
Fri. & Sat. 12noon-10:30pm, Sun. 4-9pm

Mortons the Steak House
See our ad on this page
777 Northern Boulevard, Great Neck, NY 11020
516-498-2950
Amex, Diners, MasterCard, Visa
Open 7 days - Dinner / Mon.-Sat. 5pm 11pm,
Sun. 5pm-10pm
Reservations Preferred

Santorini My Love
37 Great Neck Road, Great Neck, NY 11021
516-829-4877
Greek, Filet & Whole Fish
Amex, MasterCard, Visa
Closed Mondays
Lunch / Tues.-Fri. 11:30-4pm
Dinner Served Every Day 4-10pm
Reservations Recommended for Large Parties

Seed
See our ad on page XVII
25 Middle Neck Road, Great Neck, NY 11021
516-773-3690
Fresh American
Amex, Diners, MasterCard, Visa
Open 7 days / Mon.-Wed. 11am-10pm
Thurs. & Fri. 11am-11pm
Sat. 12noon-12am, Sun 4pm-10pm / Reservations
Recommended on Thurs., Fri., Sat. & Large Parties

Celebrating Our 50th Anniversary

FREDRICKS

Fredricks takes this opportunity to sincerely thank
it's friends and patrons for 50 wonderful years,
and in appreciation, will offer dinner specials at 1950 prices.

DINNER SPECIALS

SERVED MONDAY THRU SATURDAY, FROM 5PM TO 9:30PM

Meatloaf Platter......$3.95
with potato & vegetable

Veal Parmigiana......$3.95
with spaghetti

Baked Chicken......$3.95
with potato & vegetable

Chicken Parmigiana....$3.95
with spaghetti

Knockwurst......$2.95
with sauerkraut

Chopped Sirloin Steak...$3.95
with potato & vegetable

Meatballs...................$3.50
with spaghetti

Hebrew National Franks....$2.95
with baked beans

Filet of Flounder......$3.95
with potato & vegetable

Fishcakes......$3.95
with spaghetti

Chicken Tenders....$3.95
with french fries

Hot Turkey Platter......$3.95
with potato & vegetable

Coffee Shop

MAGAZINE
Over 2500
TITLES

FINE CIGARS

14 GRACE AVENUE, GREAT NECK, NY 11021

(516) 487-5437

Vespa

See our ad on page 138
96 Northern Boulevard, Great Neck, NY 11021
516-829-0005

Northern Italian

Amex, Diners, MasterCard, Visa
Lunch / Mon.-Fri. 12-3pm, Dinner / 4pm-Closing,
Saturday Dinner Only / 4pm to Closing, Sunday Closed
Reservations Recommended Fri. & Sat.

Wild Ginger

See our ad on page XV
48 Great Neck Road, Great Neck, NY 11022
516-487-8288

Pan Asian Cuisine

Amex, MasterCard, Visa,
Lunch / Mon.-Sat. 12noon-3:30pm
Dinner / Mon.-Thurs. 5-10:30pm,
Fri. & Sat., 5-11:30pm, Sun. 3-10pm / Reservations
Recommended Fri., Sat. & Large Parties

BAGELS / DELI

Bagel Hut

See our ad on this page
503 Middle Neck Road, Great Neck, NY 11023
516-482-8939

Bagel Mentch

See our ad on page 144
176 Middle Neck Road, Great Neck, NY 11021
516-487-BAGEL (2243)

Best Bagels

See our ad on page 144
40 Middle Neck Road, Great Neck, NY 11021
516-482-9860

Deli On The Green

See our ad on this page
647 Middle Neck Road, Great Neck, NY 11023
516-487-7440

BAKERY / CONFECTIONARY

Bruce's Restaurant & Bakery

See our ad on page 139
34 Middle Neck Road, Great Neck, NY 11021
516-829-CAKE (2253)

BEVERAGE

Little Neck Beverage

See our ad on this page
973 Northern Blvd., Great Neck, NY 11021
516-365-1280

FOOD SPECIALTY

Marine Fisheries, Inc. & Gourment

See our ad on page 145
521 Middle Neck Road, Great Neck, NY 11023
516-487-3145

Poultry Mart

See our ad on page 135,145
33 Middle Neck Road, Great Neck, NY 11021
516-487-7150

APPAREL / SHOES

Beltrami *A Men's Store*
See our ad on page 147
100 Middle Neck Road, Great Neck, NY 11021
516-466-0117

The Clog Shop
See our ad on this page
61 Middle Neck Road, Great Neck, NY 11021
516-829-7770

Jildor
See our ad on page 148
42A Middle Neck Road, Great Neck, NY 11021
516-487-6464

My Daughters Wedding III
See our ad on page 149
37 Middle Neck Road, Great Neck, NY 11021
516-773-7778

Postur-line Shoes
See our ad on page 148
40 Middle Neck Road, Great Neck, NY 11021
516-829-3505

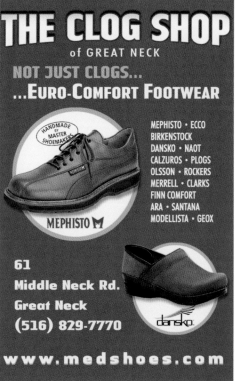

BELTRAMI

A Men's Store
Classic Italian Clothing

Mr. Ben, Proprietor
Serving Great Neck & Vicinity Since 1980

Suits • Sports Jackets • Slacks • Outerwear • Sportswear • Furnishings • Shoes

Sizes Available:
Regular • Short • Long & Portly
from 38 Short to 52 Long

Complete Tuxedo Department

Special Orders Accepted
Major Credit Cards

516.466.0117

100 MIDDLE NECK ROAD • GREAT NECK • NEW YORK

Yanni's Furs
See our ad on page XX
130 Middle Neck Road, Great Neck, NY 11021
516-504-1113

CIGARS / TOBACCO

Tobacco Plaza Ltd.
See our ad on this page
218 Lakeville Road #3, Great Neck, NY 11020
516-829-7134

Fredricks
See our ad on page 142
14 Grace Avenue, Great Neck, NY 11021
516-487-5437

GIFTS

The Culinary Connection
See our ad on page 149
10 Grace Avenue, Great Neck, NY 11021
516-829-6883

My Daughter's

(516) 773-7778

37 SOUTH MIDDLE NECK ROAD, GREAT NECK

EYEWEAR

London Optical
See our ad on this page
46 Middle Neck Road, Great Neck, NY 11021
516-487-8866

JEWELERY

Jewels by Viggi
See our ad on page XXII, 90, BC
65 Middle Neck Road, Great Neck, NY 11021
516-829-6161

KNITTING / NEEDLEPOINT

The Open Door to Stitchery
See our ad on page 150
87A Middle Neck Road, Great Neck, NY 11021
516-487-9442

PETS

Happy Tails
See our ad on this page
27 Middle Neck Road, Great Neck, NY 11021
516-466-3701

GREAT NECK
**HEALTH
&
BEAUTY**

ACUPUNCTURE

The Great Neck Wellness Center
See our ad on page 154
230 Middle Neck Road, Suite 1
Great Neck, NY 11021
516-504-4040

CHIROPRACTIC

Back To Life Chiropractic, P.C.
See our ad on page 153
21 Barstow Road, Unit 1H
Great Neck, NY 11021
516-482-7110

Bottari Chiropractic
See our ad on page 155
20 Park Place, Great Neck, NY 11021
516-466-7744

Drell Chiropractic Office
See our ad on page 156
15 Bond Street, Suite 105, Great Neck, NY 11021
516-482-4088

Dr. Joseph Debe
See our ad on page 155
38 Great Neck Road, Great Neck, NY 11021
516-829-1515

Great Neck Better Health Chiropractic
See our ad on page 153
5 Bond Street, Great Neck, NY 11021
516-829-8099

The Great Neck Wellness Center
See our ad on page 154
230 Middle Neck Road, Suite1
Great Neck, NY 11021
516-504-4040

DENTAL

Distinctive Dental Services of New York, P.C.
See our ad on page 157
173 East Shore Road, Suite 201
Great Neck, NY 11023
516-487-8110

153

Dr. Maritza Villamar, Dentist
See our ad on this this page
1 Barstow Road, Suite P-1B
Great Neck, NY 11021
516-482-4914

North Shore Cosmetic & Implant Dental
See our ad on page 156
1 Barstow Road, Suite P-18
Great Neck, NY 11021
516-877-SMILEDOC - or - 516-482-2213

Robert H. Panzer, D.D.S. Great Neck Orthrodontic Group
See our ad on this page
23 Bond Street, Great Neck, NY 11021
516-487-7475

EUROPEAN WEIGHT LOSS / SPA

VivinLinea Center Italian Weight Loss Spa
See our ad on page 158
200 Middle Neck Road, Great Neck, NY 11021
516-466-3636

FITNESS CENTERS

30 Minute Fitness
See our ad on page 161
552 Middle Neck Road, Great Neck, NY 11023
516-466-8410

Hard To Hold
See our ad on page 160
128 Middle Neck Road, Great Neck, NY 11021
516-498-9500

North Shore Fitness Clubs
See our ad on page XVII, 159
38 Great Neck Road, Great Neck, NY 11021
516-773-4888

Pilates Fitness
See our ad on this page
38 Great Neck Road, Great Neck, NY 11021
516-466-7764

Power House Pilates
See our ad on page 158
21 East Shore Road, Manhasset, NY 11030
516-365-2800

HAIR SALONS/SPAS

de-al Salon
See our ad on page XXII
91 Middle Neck Road, Great Neck, NY 11021
516-466-0340

DeFranco Spagnolo Salon & Day Spa
See our ad on page XIX, 163
200 Middle Neck Road, Great Neck, NY 11021
516-466-6752

Gustav Rouff Hair Salon
See our ad on this page
770 Middle Neck Road, Great Neck, NY 11021
516-829-5088

Dedicated to the Fine Art Fashion of Hair Design and Beauty

9 Bond Street • Great Neck • (516) 482-9060

ICON Lifestyle Salon & Spa
See our ad on page 165
44 Great Neck Road, Great Neck, NY 11021
516-829-2898

New York Hair Salon & Spa
See our ad on page 164
1 South Middle Neck Road
Great Neck, NY 11021
516-482-9016

VS1 Salon
See our ad on this page
9 Bond Street, Great Neck, NY 11021
516-482-9060

NUTRITIONIST

Dr. Joseph Debe
See our ad on page 155
38 Great Neck Road, Great Neck, NY 11021
516-829-1515

ICON

an AVEDA Concept Salon & Spa

At
ICON,
beauty,
fashion
and
wellness
become
art.

Our
team
provides
personal
attention
to your
hair,
skin,
body
and
lifestyle.

Gardens *of* Great Neck
44 Great Neck Road
Great Neck, NY 11021

516.829.2898

AVEDA.
the art and science of pure flower and plant essences

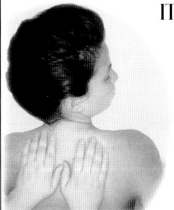
PHYSICIANS / PSYCHOLOGIST / PODIATRISTS

Great Neck Family Foot Care

See our ad on page 166
7 Bond Street, Great Neck, NY 11021
516-482-5999

Dr. Karen L. Siegel, PH.D.

See our ad on page 166
444 Community Drive, Manhasset, NY 11030
516-627-7070

Long Island Audiology

See our ad on page 162
1000 Northern Blvd., Great Neck, NY 11021
516-482-0660

THERAPEUTIC MASSAGE

Health Touch

See our ad on this page
567 Middle Neck Road, Great Neck, NY 11023
516-466-6642

VITAMINS & HEALTH FOOD

Healthy Approach

10 Bond Street, Great Neck, NY 11021
516-487-8876
Discount Vitamins, Homeopathics, Certified Nutritionist

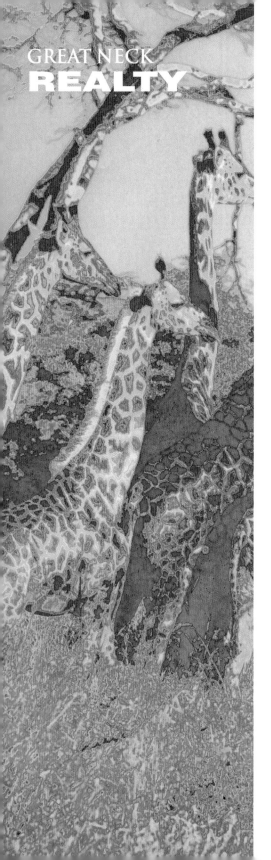

MAJESTIC

PROPERTY AFFILIATES INC.

Serving the Long Island Business Community Since 1972

Specializing in Office / Retail & Industrial Leasing & Sales

Investment Sales   Property Management   Tenant Representation

---

OFFICE · MEDICAL
PROFESSIONAL SPACE
RETAIL & INDUSTRIAL

PRIME BUILDINGS & LOCATIONS
550-100,000 SQUARE FEET

GREAT NECK & VICINITY · NASSAU · SUFFOLK · NORTH SHORE · SOUTH SHORE · QUEENS

Garden City · Glen Cove · Great Neck · Jericho · Manhasset · New Hyde Park
Roslyn · Westbury · Syosset · Melville · Rockville Centre · Franklin Square · Greenvale
Elmont · Lake Success · Lynbrook · Mineola · Port Washington · Valley Stream

> ### MAJESTIC is #1 Across L.I.
> ### Call Your Commercial Space Specialist...
> ### Your Source!!!

MAJESTIC Property Affiliates, Inc.

www.officespacelongisland.com

60 CUTTER MILL ROAD · GREAT NECK · (516) 466-310
Robert Huhem-President

APPELMAN LERNER
REAL ESTATE, INC.

THE VARIETY OF OUR EXCLUSIVE LISTINGS IS EXCEEDED ONLY BY THE QUALITY OF OUR EXCEPTIONAL TEAM.

Ilse Appelman · *Sandra Lerner*

MARIA DILMANIAN · PAULA CRANE · MIRIAM HENDLER · JANE COHEN
JANET KASHANI · IMA LAVI · CAROLYN LIU · IRAJ KASHANI
JACKIE MALEKAN · JANE SACHS · JENNIFER VERDICCHIO · LEAH ZAR
KATHY CANCELLIERE · CARYL SHAPIRO · WENDY SHAPIRO
LILIAN SCHUSTER · TOBY PERLIN

PHONE: 516.482.1230
FAX: 516.482.1298

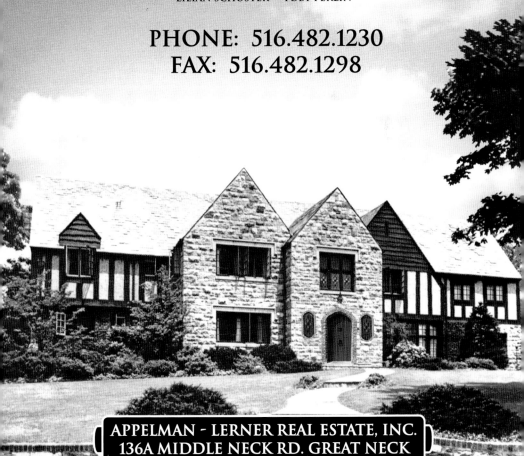

APPELMAN - LERNER REAL ESTATE, INC.
136A MIDDLE NECK RD. GREAT NECK

Property Profiles, Inc.
See our ad on this page
63 Cutter Mill Road, Great Neck, NY 11021
516-773-2400

Trylon Realty
See our ad on page 173
167 Middle Neck Road, Great Neck, NY 11021
516-482-8400

Turn Key Real Estate
See our ad on page IFC
7 Bond Street, Great Neck, NY 11021
516-829-2205

REAL ESTATE MANAGEMENT COMPANYS

Richland Management
See our ad on page 174
10 Welwyn Road, Great Neck, NY 11021
516-487-2912

Schalit Management Associates, Ltd.
See our ad on page 174
One Linden Place, Suite 410
Great Neck, NY 11021
516-466-3377

Advance
Abstract
Corporation
Celebrates

20 Years
of Service
to the
Real Estate,
Legal & Banking
Communities

We Deliver Title Services on Time All the Time

- Title Insurance

- Closing and
  Settlement Services

- Foreclosure
  Certification

- Cooperative Searches

- Tax and Lien
  Searches

- Surveys and
  Appraisal (by
  Licensed Associates)

- Entire States of
  New York and
  New Jersey

- National Accounts

- Underwritten by
  Four National
  Underwriters

Advance
Abstract
Corporation

Headquaters:
New York:
560 Northern Blvd., Suite 200
Great Neck, NY 11021
Tel: 516-482-9050
        718-639-1224
        914-997-2787
Fax: 516-482-9348

New Jersey:
P.O. Box 1911
Bloomfield, NJ 07003
Tel: 973-429-7722
Fax: 516-482-9348

E-mail: info@advanceabstract.com

Member: American Land Title Association, New York Land Title Association,
New Jersey Land Title Association, Long Island Builders Institute, Long Island Association

175

GREAT NECK
HOME

DECORATIVE DOOR & CABINET HARDWARE / PLUMBING FITTINGS

Kolson Korenge, Inc.
See our ad on page 177
653 Middle Neck Road, Great Neck, NY 11023
516-487-1224

ELECTRICAL

Great Neck Electric Co., Inc.
See our ad on page 180
245 East Shore Road, Great Neck, NY 11023
516-482-3030

JHACS Electric
See our ad on page 180
611 Middle Neck Road, Great Neck, NY 11023
516-773-8000

EXTERMINATING

Arrow Exterminating Co., Inc.
See our ad on page 132
www.arrowexterminating.com
516-829-1777

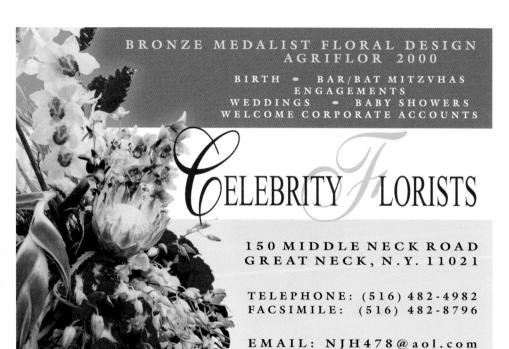
FAUX FINISHING

Special Decorative Surface Design
See our ad on page 176
Great Neck, NY 11023
516-829-7277

FLORIST

Celebrity Florist
See our ad on this page
150 Middle Neck Road, Great Neck, NY 11021
516-482-4982

FOR THE HOME

The Frame Factory Ltd.
See our ad on page 180
733 Middle Neck Road, Great Neck, NY 11024
516-482-7446

Inter-Marble, Inc.
See our ad on page 177
334 Northern Blvd., Great Neck, NY 11021
516-829-3570

Sid Hall Floors
See our ad on page 181
106 Northern Blvd., Great Neck, NY 11021
516-487-5591

The Tint Shop
See our ad on page 181
135 Cutter Mill Road, Great Neck, NY 11021
516-829-7336

HEATING / AIR CONDITIONING

Systematic Control Corp.
See our ad on page XIV, IBC
92 Northern Boulevard, Great Neck, NY 11021
516-482-1375

PLUMBING / HEATING SUPPLIES

See next page

179

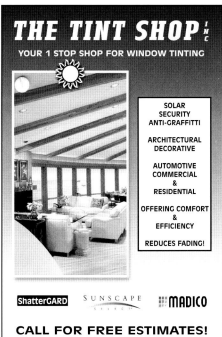

GREAT NECK PROFESSIONAL & BUSINESS SERVICES

ACCOUNTANT

Elliot S. Rosenblatt CPA, MBA
83 Middle Neck Road Great Neck, NY 11021
516-466-2292

ARCHITECTS

Guilor Architects
See our ad on page 183
249 Northern Blvd., Great Neck, NY 11021
516-482-6777

Frank Richard Gencorelli: A.I.A., Architect
See our ad on page 135
8 Bond Street, Great Neck, NY 11021
516-487-4465

ATTORNEYS

Law Office of Gerald M. Oginski, L.L.C.
See our ad on page 183
150 Great Neck Road, Suite 304
Great Neck, NY 11021
516-487-8207

The Law Offices of Michael J. Motelson
See our ad on page 184
134 Middle Neck Road, Suite 200
Great Neck, NY 11021
516-487-7077

Sharon Kovacs Gruer, Attorney at Law
See our ad on page 184
1010 Northern Blvd., Great Neck, NY 11021
516-466-WILL - or - 516-487-5400

BANKING / FINANCE / DEPOSITORY

Astoria Federal Savings
See our ad on page 185
4 Great Neck Road, Great Neck, NY 11021
516-487-9300

North Fork Bank
See our ad on page 185
60 Cutter Mill Road, Great Neck, NY 11021
516-773-1880

183

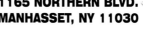

See page 188

Great Neck Plaza Management Council
See our ad on page 187
72 Middle Neck Road, Great Neck, NY 11021
516-829-1301

CELLULAR PHONES

Direct Page & Cellular
See our ad on page 187
9 Great Neck Road, Great Neck, NY 11021
516-482-4616

COMPUTERS

Great Neck Computers
See our ad on page 189
57A Cutter Mill Road, Great Neck, NY 11021
516-773-8560

DRY CLEANING

Nu-Clear Cleaners
See our ad on this page
172 Middle Neck Road, Great Neck, NY 11021
516-482-8905

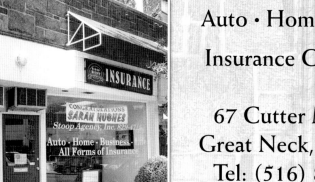

PRINTING / COPYING / PHOTO

Advantage Print & Mail Services, Inc.
See our ad on page 190
15 Cutter Mill Road, Suite 177
Great Neck, NY 11021
516-334-2759

Hi Tech Photo Imaging
See our ad on page 192
36 Middle Neck Road, Great Neck, NY 11021
516-466-5885

Plaza Printing · Copying
See our ad on this page
124 Northern Blvd., Great Neck, NY 11021
516-487-1600

Sir Speedy
See our ad on this page
81 Cutter Mill Road, Great Neck, NY 11021
516-829-5300

When you look good people notice

- Newsletters
- Catalogues
- Brochures
- Manuals
- Copies
- Direct Mailing
- Stationery
- Full Bindery

Sir Speedy
PRINTING • COPYING • DIGITAL NETWORK
81 Cutter Mill Road, Great Neck, New York 11021
(800) 281-4199 • www.sirspeedy.com/greatneck

PLAZA PRINTING COPYING

GREAT NECK'S FULL SERVICE PRINTER SINCE 1973

OFFSET PRINTING
DIGITAL XEROX COPIES
COLOR LASER COPIES
FAX SERVICE

Commercial Stationery & Business Cards
Typesetting & Design - PC & Mac Capabilities
Print From Your Disk / CD • Large Document Copying
Custom Forms Design & Printing

Medical / Legal / Real Estate Specialists
Mailing & List Maintenance • Full Bindery
High Speed Scanning to Disc • Labels • NCR Sets
Document Shredding • Self Inking Stamps

124 NORTHERN BLVD. GREAT NECK
Fax: 516.487.8646   Email: info@plazagn.com
516.487.1600

TITLE COMPANY

Advance Abstract Corp.
See our ad on page 175
560 Northern Blvd, Suite 200
Great Neck, NY 11021
516-482-9050

STORAGE

Shurgard
See our ad on page 193
91 Cutter Mill Road, Great Neck, NY 11021
516-466-2542

Westy's Storage Centers
See our ad on page XVI
2400 Marcus Avenue, Lake Sucess, NY 11042
516-327-5000

Here are 50% more reasons to come to Shurgard.

If you want safe, convenient storage, come to Shurgard. We have 24-hour video surveillance, climate controlled units, and access from 7 a.m. to 10 p.m. We also offer a wide selection of packing supplies, and we'll even accept deliveries. Right now we'll also take 50% off your first month's rent.

SHURGARD S T O R A G E CENTER

www.shurgard.com

Expect **more.**

Shurgard of Great Neck • 91 Cuttermill Rd. • 516-504-0974

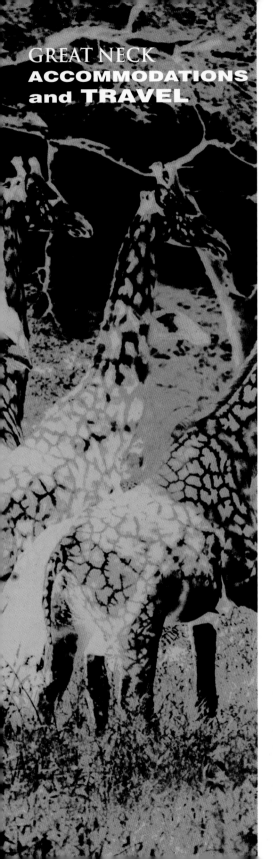

GREAT NECK
ACCOMMODATIONS
and TRAVEL

ACCOMODATIONS

The Andrew
See our ad on page 195
75 North Station Plaza, Great Neck NY 11021
516-482-2900 - or 1-866-THE-ANDREW

Inn at Great Neck
See our ad on page XXV
30 Cutter Mill Road, Great Neck, NY 11021
516-773-2000

TRAVEL

Travel Express International Limited
See our ad on this page
Atrium Building
98 Cutter Mill Road, Great Neck, NY 11021
516-482-1717

T.R.I.P. Tours
See our ad on page 195
60 Cutter Mill Road, Suite 214
Great Neck, NY 11021
516-487-9400

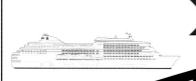

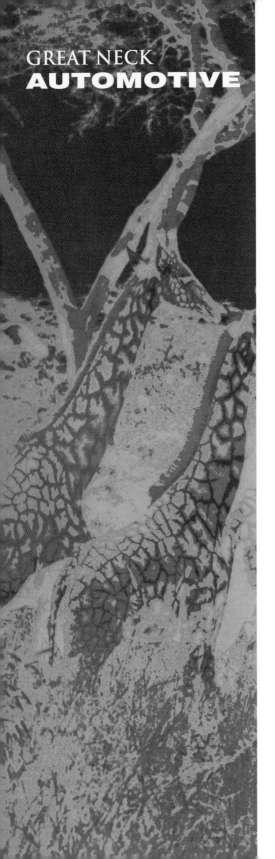

GREAT NECK
AUTOMOTIVE

AUTO REPAIR

Aero Auto Body
See our ad on this page
135 Cutter Mill Road, Great Neck, NY 11021
516-482-9700

All County Auto Glass
See our ad on page 197
325 Great Neck Road, Great Neck, NY 11021
516-466-0001

Automotive Workshop
See our ad on page 198
385 Great Neck Road, Great Neck, NY 11021
516-482-7030

Euro-Tech Collision
See our ad on page 200
325 Great Neck Road, Great Neck, NY 11021
516-829-5880

Great Neck Collision
See our ad on page 200
1 Elm Street, Great Neck, NY 11021
516-829-9499

Norman Collision Works
See our ad on page 197
362-363 Great Neck Rd, Great Neck, NY 11021
516-466-3933

NORMAN COLLISION WORKS

AUTO BODY • UNIBODY REPAIRS

Telephone
(516) 466-3933

362 Great Neck Road, Great Neck • New York

AUTO DEALERSHIPS

Biener Nissan Audi
See our ad on page 198
795-803 Northern Blvd., Great Neck, NY 11021
Nissan - 516-482-7700
Audi - 516-829-2834

North Bay Cadillac
See our ad on page 199
730 Northern Blvd., Great Neck, NY 11021
516-466-6200

North Shore Infinity of Great Neck
See our ad on page 199
720 Northern Blvd., Great Neck, NY 11021
516-773-1000

Jaguar of Great Neck Roslyn
See our ad on page 199
732 Northern Blvd., Great Neck, NY 11021
516-482-5500

Manhasset Mitsubishi
See our ad on page 198
1225 Northern Blvd., Great Neck, NY 11030
516-365-7300

AUTO ACCESSORIES/ CUSTOM SERVICES

Blazing Sound & Performance
See our ad on page 200
195 Northern Blvd., Great Neck, NY 11021
516-773-4349

Great Neck Car Wash & Detailing
See our ad on page 133
790 Northern Blvd., Great Neck, NY 11021
516-466-0002

Parts & Polish Motor Sport Accessories
See our ad on page 201
556 Northern Blvd., Great Neck, NY 11021
516-466-3553

The Tint Shop
See our ad on page 181
135 Cutter Mill Road, Great Neck, NY 11021
516-829-7336

CAR WASH

Great Neck Car Wash & Detailing
See our ad on page 133
790 Northern Blvd., Great Neck, NY 11021
516-466-0002

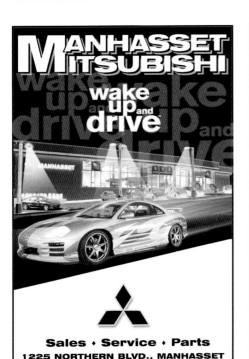

The Road to Luxury Leads to Great Neck.

- ■ A 63 Year History of Trust in the Commmunity.
- ■ The Most Aggressive Pricing in New York.
- ■ New and Pre-Owned Available.

New York State's
#1 Volume
Cadillac Dealer.

In1938,
We were the First,..
Today the BEST.

Long Island's
Exclusive North
Shore Infiniti Dealer.

730 Northern Blvd
Great Neck 516.466.6200

732 Northern Blvd
Great Neck 516.482.5500

720 Northern Blvd
Great Neck 516.773.1000

CEC ▪ AC Schnitzer ▪ Antera ▪ Lorinser ▪ Remus ▪ Azev ▪ TechArt ▪ Victor ▪ TTE
556 NORTHERN BLVD. GREAT NECK. N.Y. 11021

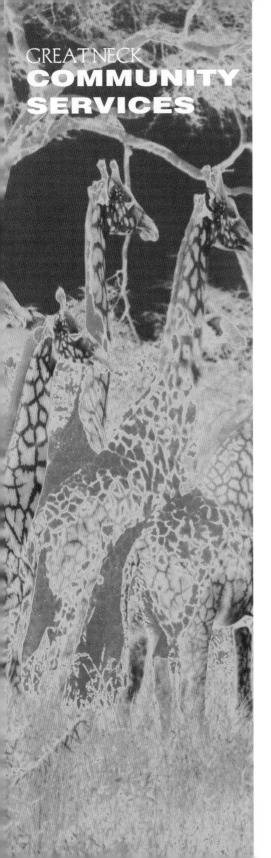

CHILD CARE / EDUCATION

(Early Childhood Education)

CLASP Children's Center
See our ad on page 203
80 Grace Avenue, Great Neck, NY 11021
516-482-8090

Great Neck Community School
See our ad on page 203
225 Schenck Avenue, Great Neck, NY 11021
516-482-5005

Gymboree Play & Music
See our ad on page 204
The Courtyard, Upper Level
770 Middle Neck Road, Great Neck, NY 11024
516-466-1308

The Learning Window -
A Childrens Center
See our ad on page 203
241 Shoreward Drive, Great Neck, NY 11021
516-487-5584

HEALTH CARE / ASSISTED LIVING FACILITIES

Atria Assisted Living
See our ad on page 205
51 Great Neck Road, Great Neck, NY 11021
516-829-4100

COPAY, Inc. (Non-Profit)
See our ad on page 204
21 North Station Road, Great Neck, NY 11021
516-466-2509

The Grace Plaza of Great Neck
See our ad on page 206
15 St. Pauls Place, Great Neck, NY 11021
516-466-3001

Heart To Home, Inc.
See our ad on page 204
401 Great Neck Road, Great Neck, NY 11021
516-829-6000

The Mayfair of Great Neck
See our ad on page 207
96 Cutter Mill Road, Great Neck, NY 11021
1-888-778-1370

NON-PROFIT ORGANIZATIONS

CLASP
See our ad on page 203
80 Grace Avenue, Great Neck, NY 11021
516-482-8090

COPAY, Inc. (Non-Profit)
See our ad on this page
21 North Station Road, Great Neck, NY 11021
516-466-2509

Great Neck United Community Fund
See our ad on page 207
30 Cumberland Avenue, Great Neck, NY 11020
516-482-8101

FUNERAL HOME

Riverside - Nassau North Chapels
See our ad on page 205
55 North Station Plaza, Great Neck, NY 11021
516-487-9600

"PATHWAYS"
to
Recovery & Independance
...a Reputation for Success.

"PATHWAYS" SUBACUTE PROGRAM

Short Term Rehabilitation
Post Surgical Care
Orthopedic / Cardiac Rehabilitation
Total Joint Replacement Program

"Our Neighborhood"
Cognitive Retraining
Program

Complex Medical Care
IV Therapy
Total Parenteral Nutrition
Tracheostomy Care
Peritoneal Dialysis
Pain Management

Vascular Rehabilitation
Program
Wound Care
Diabetes Management
Amputee / Prosthetic Mgmt

LONG TERM CARE

Skilled Nursing Services
"The Heritage" Dedicated
Alzheimer's Unit
*Most Insurance Accepted

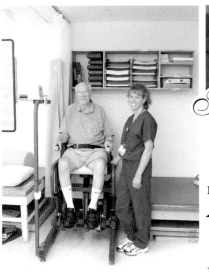

ESTABLISHED 1972

The Grace Plaza
of Great Neck

REHABILITATION & NURSING CENTER

(516) 466-3001

WWW.GRACEPLAZA.COM
E-MAIL: GRACEPLAZA@AOL.COM

15 ST. PAUL'S PLACE, GREAT NECK, N.Y. 11021

Local Organizations

Chamber of Commerce

Kiosk Information Center / 1 Middle Neck Road,
Mailing address / 643 Middle Neck Road,
Great Neck, New York 11023
Elliot S. Rosenblatt, president (516) 487-2000
www.greatneckchamber.org
or email info@greatneckchamber.org

The Great Neck Chamber of Commerce is a 350-plus member business organization and is one of the largest and most active Chambers in Nassau County. Its mission is to unify the retail, commercial, industrial and service businesses of Great Neck, as well as the professional leaders and institutions of the community. The Chamber promotes business with the goal of increasing sales for retail and commercial business establishments. It monitors the progress of Great Neck business, large and small, and advances the mutual interests through study, research, contact with elected officials, legislation and information and services.

Chamber of Commerce Executive Committee - From left to right - Anthony N. Carbone, Carol A. Anderson, David L. Lurie, Elliot S. Rosenblatt, Robert L. Goldfarb, Valerie A. Link, Steven J. Tuchler, Suzette A. Gray. Ronald A. Samanowitz (not pictured).

The Chamber invests in the economic growth and development of Great Neck, and shares a strong commitment to the business community with the common objective to make the Great Neck peninsula a great and prosperous place to live, work and shop.

The Chamber publishes a monthly newsletter, the S.I.G.N. Post, presents the Giraffe Award to those individuals "who stick their neck out for Great Neck," conducts ribbon-cuttings for new businesses, has monthly networking breakfasts and many other business, village and social activities.

President
Elliot S. Rosenblatt, CPA
Rosenblatt and Associates

First Vice President
Carol A. Anderson
Advantage Print & Mail Services

Second Vice President
Anthony N. Carbone
Systematic Control Corp

Third Vice President
Valerie A. Link
Great Neck Record/Anton Publications

Secretary
Suzette A. Gray
Merrill Lynch

Treasurer
Steven J. Tuchler
North Fork Bank

Administrative Secretary
David L. Lurie
Lurie Realty Corp.

Immediate Past President
Robert L. Goldfarb, CPA
Schoenfeld Mendelsohn Goldfarb LLP

Counsel
Ronald A. Samanowitz, Esq.
Samanowitz & Endzweig

Office Secretary
Ronit Weiss

Board Of Directors

Peter Andreasian
Andreasian Property Management Co.
Daniel Arbusman
Jewels by Viggi Ltd.
Phil Bee
Great Neck News/Litmor Publishing Corp.
Marilyn Benson
Anton Publications
Paula R. Blumen
T.R.I.P. Tours

Hon. Ed Causin
Mayor - Village of Great Neck Estates

Hon. Jean Celender
Mayor - Village of Great Neck Plaza

John Dominsky
Village of Great Neck

Janet Eshagoff
June Shapiro Realty Fine Homes and Estates

Regina Gil
GN Center for Visual & Performing Arts

Joseph Kapner, CPA
L. Belgraier, CPA PC

Steven Kocoris
North Fork Bank

Leigh Laitinen
Advantage Print & Mail Services

Michael Larkin
*United Community Fund of Great Neck and
North New Hyde Park*

Judy Litner
Travel Express International Ltd

Neil Marrin
Great Neck Park District

Dr. Daniel Matzner
Great Neck Better Health Chiropractic

John Meitner
Salomon Smith Barney

Alan Mindel
Inn at Great Neck

Henry Nemat
Nemat Homes

Sheila Penn
FOCUS, Inc.

Jeffrey Phillips
Cafe Rustica

Philip Raices
Turn Key Real Estate

Pasquale "Pat" Riccardi
Sir Speedy

Joe Rosenberg
Mail Boxes, Etc.

Walter L. Roth
Great Neck Properties Company

Hon. J. Leonard Samansky
Village of Saddle Rock

Lee Seeman
Tri-Northern Insurance Group

Richard Stancati
Melville Hall, USMMA

Judy Stern
Organize NOW

Carol Teplin
Village of Great Neck Plaza

Rosa Toong
Waldbaums

Muriel Turk
Great Neck Library

Joan Ucinski
Astoria Federal Savings & Loan

Joan Wheeler
JLW Creative Services

Howard Zwang
Best Tire Alignment Corp

Past Presidents

Jesse M. Markel*	Howard Leeds
Willis H. Bryant*	Jeffery A. Kushner
Leon K. Shanack*	David L. Lurie
Howard L. Friend*	Marilyn Benson
Arnold B. Prensky*	Robert L. Goldfarb

* Deceased

Not-For-Profit Organizations

United Community Fund

30 Cumberland Avenue, Great Neck, NY 11020
516-482-8101
"Neighbors helping Neighbors." UCF is a grass-roots organization that raises funds for 14 member organizations that serve the Great Neck peninsula. Social, medical and other human services help improve quality of life for all.

COPAY, The Community Organization for Parents and Youth

21 North Station Road, Great Neck, NY 11021
516-466-2509
Community based bilingual human services agency provides counseling services for families, individuals and children and significant others. Its primary focus is the professional treatment and prevention of drug addiction and alcoholism. New York State-licensed as a 1035 outpatient medically managed intensive care facility. Goal is to help attain sobriety and develop a sober life style.

Manhasset-Great Neck EOC, Economic Opportunity Council

65 High Street
Manhasset, NY 11030
516-627-1750

Sponsors the local Head Start program, supervised recreational activities, learning opportunities for grade school children and a summer youth program are offered, along with academic and job training for youth, plus adult service; FEMA, resume writing and job training.

Girl Scouts of Nassau County, Inc.

Roosevelt Field
110 Ring Road W,
Garden City, NY 11530
516-741-2550

"Where Girls Grow Strong." Educational and recreational activities for girls ages 5 to 18. Girls learn to grow and develop into responsible adults and productive members of their community and discover the fun, friendship and power of girls together.

Great Neck Student Aid Fund Inc.

P.O. Box 1067, Great Neck NY 11023
516-829-9437

Helps Great Neck students with financial support for their first year of college through outright grants.

Womanspace

3 St. Paul's Place, Great Neck NY 11021
516-829-6566

A women's center which provides support and referral service, activities for women including memoir writing and poetry, yoga, support groups and discussion groups linking women to the community and to other women as well as advocating for the equality of opportunity for all women. The Independent Business Women's Circle serves the needs of women in business.

CLASP Children's Center

80 Grace Avenue, Great Neck, NY 11021
516-482-8090

Children's Living After School Program. Before and after school care and after camp care in summer for children of working parents is provided for K-5. Also offers a full-day, 12-month Early Childhood program children ages 18 months to 4 years. An intergenerational program facilitates interaction and activities between seniors and children.

Child Abuse Prevention Services (CAPS)

P.O. Box 176, Roslyn, NY 11576
516-621-0552

Dedicated to preventing child abuse and neglect through community awareness and school educational programs.

Great Neck Senior Center

80 Grace Avenue, Great Neck, NY 11021
516-487-0025

Multi-purpose center offering a variety of educational, recreational and cultural activities for senior adults such as exercise aerobics, yoga, tai chi, dance, bridge, holistic health, trips to museums, theaters and concerts. Counseling, bereavement and caregivers groups and social service information is available. A nutritious hot lunch and transportation is provided five days a week.

Sara's Center

781 Middle Neck Rd, Great Neck, NY 11024
516-482-1550

Wellness education and treatment through the arts. A community based day treatment alternative to traditional, institutional models of care. Therapies combined with functional skill development create a holistic model of care for people living with special needs including mental illness.

Nassau County Coalition Against Domestic Violence

250 Fulton Avenue, Hempstead NY 11550
516-572-0700

Crisis service for victims of domestic violence and rape, including 24-hour, 7-day per week hotlines (516-542-0404/domestic violence; 516-222-2293/rape), emergency safe housing, legal consultation, individual and group counseling, educational presentations for schools and community, training for professionals in the area of domestic violence, elder abuse and sexual assault.

Great Neck Visiting Nurse Association

41 Mirrilees Circle, Great Neck NY 11021
516-739-1270

Professional nursing staff supplies in-home nursing care; rehabilitation services; physical, occupational and speech therapy; home health aides; nursing home assessment; nutritional counseling, Meals-on-Wheels program delivers nourishing meals to shut-ins; all meals are prepared to conform to the dietary requirements of the clients. Free dental care is available to needy schoolchildren. Co-sponsors Open Door Parent-Child Caring Center that offers families with children under five professional counseling.

North Shore Child and Family Guidance
480 Old Westbury Rd, Roslyn Height, NY 11577
516-626-1971
"Caring for the Emotional Health of Our Communities." The center offers a wide range of mental health services to children, youth and families including diagnostics assessments, individual, family and group therapy; psycho-educational assessment and treatment; substance abuse services; bereavement and trauma services, and special programs geared to issues such as single parenting, early childhood development and abuse prevention and treatment. The center is also a training and consultation center for parents and professionals offering workshops, community education forums, newsletters and a speakers bureau.

North Shore - Long Island Jewish Health System/ New Leadership Division/Child Life and Education Services Program
125 Community Drive, Great Neck, NY 11201
516-465-2554
Helps seriously ill hospitalized children and their families cope with the trauma of needed treatments. Children in the Hematology/Oncology, Bone Marrow Transplant, Intensive Care and general pediatric units are served.

The Salvation Army
111 Willis Avenue, Mineola NY11501
516-747-4902
Disaster assistance and financial aid are readily available with a volunteer services unit located in Great Neck. Service includes summer camp for needy youth, emergency food and clothing, hot coffee for firefighters and seasonal assistance.

Boy Scouts of Nassau County
Theodore Roosevelt Council
544 Broadway
Massapequa, NY 11758
516-796-7600
For boys 7 to 18. Educational and recreational activities. Scouting encourages youth to develop new skills, become more self-reliant and learn the value of helping others.

Helpful Numbers

Movie Theater
Squire Cinemas.............................466-2020
(Movie Link (777-film)

Transportation
Long Island Rail Road...................822-5477
Port Authority Bus Terminal...212-564-8484
Long Island Bus Info......................766-6722
Amtrak................................1-800-USA-RAIL

Fire Departments
Alert..487-7000
Manhasset-Lakeville.......................466-4411
Vigilant...482-5000

Great Neck Police Departments
Great Neck Estates.......................487-7700
Kensington.....................................482-0480
Kings Point....................................482-1000
Lake Success...............................482-4600

Nassau County Police Departments
6th Precinct...911
Non-Emergency 573-6600

Ambulance
North of RR Tracks:
Vigilant 482-5000
South of RR Tracks:
Manhasset-Lakeville.......................466-4411

Gas/Electric/Water
LIPA/KEYSPAN
Customer Service..................800-490-0025
LIPA Electric Service..............800-490-0075
KEYSPAN Gas Emergency Only
....800-490-0045
Water Authority of Great Neck North:
    Office 487-7973
    Emergency............................482-0210
Manhasset-Lakeville Water
District..466-4416

Great Neck Public Schools

Administration

Information.....................................773-1404
Superintendent.............................773-1407
Transportation..............................773-1460
Student Registration.....................773-1459
Community Services.....................773-1456

Public

John L. Miller
North High School (9-12)
35 Polo Road, Great Neck, NY 11023
516-773-1513

South High School (9-12)
341 Lakeville Road, Great Neck, NY 11020
516-773-1602

Richard S, Sherman
North Middle School (6-8)
77 Polo Road, Great Neck NY 11023
516-773-1572

South Middle School (6-8)
349 Lakeville Road, Great Neck, NY 11020
516-773-1664

Village School (9-12)
614 Middle Neck Road., Great Neck, NY 11023
516-773-1705

Elizabeth M. Baker School (K-5)
69 Baker Hill Road, Great Neck NY 11023
516-773-1470

John F. Kennedy School (K-5)
1A Grassfield Road, Great Neck, NY 11024
516-773-1480

Lakeville School (1-5)
47-27 Jayson Avenue, Great Neck, NY 11020
516-773-1490

Lakeville Kindergarden@
Parkville (ages 3 & 4)
10 Campbell Street, New Hyde Park, NY 11040
516-773-1707

Saddle Rock Elementary
School (K-5)
10 Hawthorne Ln., Great Neck, NY 11023
516-773-1500

Adult Education

Cumberland Adult Center
30 Cumberland Avenue, Great Neck, NY 11020
516-773-1713

Clover Adult Center
105 Clover Drive, Great Neck, NY 11021
516-773-1720

Great Neck Library

Main Library
159 Bayview Avenue, Great Neck, NY 11023
516-466-8055

Lakeville Branch
475 Great Neck Road, Great Neck, NY 11021
516-466-8055 ext. 231

Station Branch
40B Great Neck Road, Great Neck, NY 11021
516-466-8055 ext. 232

Parkville Branch
10 Campbell Street, New Hyde Park, NY 11040
516-466-8055 ext. 234

Great Neck Post Offices

Main Office
1 Welwyn Road, Great Neck, NY 11021
516-482-5011

Old Village Station
661 Middle Neck Road, Great Neck, NY 11023
516-829-6315

Great Neck Park District

Park District Office
5 Beach Road, Great Neck, NY 11023
516-482-0181

Parkwood Administration Office
65 Arrandale Avenue, Great Neck, NY 11023
516-487-7665

Parkwood Sports Complex (Rink)
65 Arrandale Avenue, Great Neck, NY 11023
516-482-2975

Great Neck House
14 Arrandale Avenue, Great Neck, NY 11023
516-482-0355

Parkwood Indoor Tennis
Parkwood Tennis Learning Center
516-829-9050

Great Neck Business Organizations

Great Neck Chamber of Commerce
Kiosk / 1 Middle Neck Road,
Great Neck, NY 11021
Office / 643 Middle Neck Road
Great Neck, NY 11023
516-487-2000
www.greatneckchamber.org
www.shopingreatneck.com

G.N. Plaza Management Council (BID)
5 Bond Street, Great Neck, NY 11021
516-829-1301

Independent Business Women's Circle (IBWC)
3 St. Paul's Place, Great Neck, NY 11021
516-829-6566

Seniors

Great Neck Senior Center
80 Grace Avenue, Great Neck, NY 11021
516-487-0025
Multi-purpose center offering a variety of educational, recreational and cultural activities for senior adults such as exercise aerobics, yoga, tai chi, dance, bridge, holistic health, trips to museums, theaters and concerts. Counseling, bereavement and caregivers groups and social service information is available. A nutritious hot lunch and transportation is provided five days a week.

Meals on Wheels
100 Garden City Plaza
Garden City, NY 11050
516-739-1292
Special homebound meal delivery program providing two nutritious meals daily, five days a week. Meals delivered to qualified elderly in need of this service to delay or avoid institutionalization.

Senior Mitzva Group of Temple Isreal
108 Old Mill Road
Great Neck, NY 11201
516-482-7800
Any mature community person is welcome to join. Dance movement excercises, balanced lunch, Yiddish cultural program, and round-table dicussions. All major Jewish and American holidays celebrated by special luncheon and entertainment, art classes and music.

American Association of Retired Persons (AARP)
New York State Office
780 Third Avenue, 33rd Floor
New York, NY 10017
212-758-1411
Non-profit, nonpartisan organization with active involvement in community, state and national affairs. Numerous programs available. Medicare and Medicaid assistance.

Nassau County Dept. of Senior Citizins Affairs
1550 Franklin Avenue, 2nd floor South,
Mineola NY 11501
516-571-5814
Provides services that assist senior citizens to remain in their homes as long as possible.

ADVERTISERS INDEX

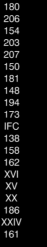

BIBLIOGRAPHY

Great Neck Circle Magazine
Great Neck News
Great Neck Record
North Hempstead Record
Newsday
The New York Times
Fitzgerald, F. Scott, Matthew J. Bruccoli, The Great Gatsby, Simon and Shuster, 1995
Great Neck Chamber of Commerce, A Complete Guide to Living and Working in Great Neck, 1996
Great Neck Estates Civic Association, Village of Great Neck Estates, 1992
Great Neck Synagogue, 50th Anniversary Journal, Spring 2001
Henry, Sondra, Temple Israel of Great Neck, The New Light, A Walking Tour of Great Neck's
 Synagogues, Fall 2000
The League of Women Voters of Great Neck, This is Great Neck, Purveyors Press, Inc. Multiple
 editions.
Mackay, Robert B. Geoffrey L. Rossano and Carol Traynor, Between Ocean & Empire: An
 Illustrated History of Long Island, Windsor Publications, 1985
Marx, Groucho, Groucho and Me, DaCapo Press,1995
Morgenstern, Mildred G. The Early History of Great Neck, Long Island, Master's Thesis, Queens
 College, 1957
Silver, Nathan, The Village of Great Neck: People Remember the Way It Was, Incorporated
 Village of Great Neck, 1996
Smith, Scottie Fitzgerald, Matthew J. Bruccoli, Joan P. Kerr, Romantic Egoists: A Pictorial
 Autobiography from the Albums of Scott and Zelda Fitzgerald, Scribner, 1974
Solomon, Nancy, Village of Great Neck Plaza Historic and Cultural Resource Survey Report, Long
 Island Traditions, Port Washington, NY, 2001
Spear, Devah and Gil, The Book of Great Neck, 1935
Swaab, Alexander M., The Long Island Story, Frank E. Richards Phoenix, NY, 1966
The Great Neck Library 1889-1989, In Celebration: The First 100 Years
Princeton University Libraries.
The Works of John Held Jr., Wes Washburn, NY 1931
Arista 1956 yearbook
Arista 1967 yearbook
Astoria Motion Picture & Television Foundation
www.pbs.org/wgbh/amex/kids/civilrights/features_hutchison.html www.lihistory.com
www.greatneckchamber.org/
www.nassaulibrary.org/gneck/
www.westegg.com/greatneck/
www.carman.net/Edith.htm
www.acun.com/dentons/Richard%20Gildersleeve.htm
www.tridget.com/lardnermania/life.htm
www.uta.edu/english/tim/baseball/lardner.html
www.accd.edu/sac/english/bailey/lardner.htm
www.greatneck.k12.ny.us/
wso.williams.edu/~dgerstei/chaplin/intro.html
www.time.com/time/time100/artists/profile/chaplin.html
www.aolsvc.worldbook.aol.com/wbol/wbAuth/jsp/wbArticle.jsp
www.hollywoodlegends.com/wc-fields.html
www.joancrawfordonline.com/index1.html
www.manhasset.org/history/cutter.html